Satiric Catharsis in Shakespeare

A THEORY OF DRAMATIC STRUCTURE

ALICE LOTVIN BIRNEY

Satiric Catharsis in Shakespeare

A THEORY OF DRAMATIC STRUCTURE

University of California Press

Berkeley · Los Angeles · London

1973

University of California Press
Berkeley and Los Angeles, California
University of California Press, Ltd.
London, England
Copyright © 1973, by
The Regents of the University of California
ISBN: 0-520-02214-9
Library of Congress Catalog Card Number: 79-185976
Printed in the United States of America

For Esther Lotvin and Adrian Birney

Contents

Preface

THIS BOOK REOPENS what is surely the most vexed subject in aesthetics; it also reinterprets aspects of two writers who have perhaps been the most overinterpreted thinkers of all times. With due apologies, then, to the tormented ghosts of Aristotle and Shakespeare, I herein reexamine the notion of dramatic catharsis in the hope that its fresh application to Shakespeare's satiric plays will justify the necessary repetitions.

The theory of satiric catharsis suggested in Chapter I is meant to be of general significance. However, I have restricted its application in this book to a representative range of those Shakespearean plays that are strongly satiric. Chapter II deals with four early history plays that include a unifying satiric character as dramatic force and culminate in the famous *Richard III*. Chapter IV, on *As You Like It*, and Chapter VI, on *Timon of Athens*, show how satiric catharsis works in a comic and tragic structure respectively. Chapters III and V examine some structures I call noncathartic in the light of their satiric protagonists, Falstaff and Thersites. The technique throughout is exegetical, which results in five readings that illustrate aspects of the theory.

Satiric catharsis, or its suppression, is an issue in all

drama that includes the element of satiric or critical attack. Although the body of this text (Chapters II–VI)
limits application of the theory to five Shakespearean
dramas, the Conclusion suggests its relevance to politically engaged drama from Aristophanes to Brecht and
his followers.

The scholarly apparatus that supports the theory and
its illustrations is intended to aid readers who are serious
students of satire or of Shakespeare. No scholar in these
areas today truthfully can claim to do exhaustive re-
search; I have tried to consider most of the major English
and American scholarship dealing with the specific issues
of satire and catharsis as related to Shakespeare through
1968. The extensive documentation should, however, not
create an impediment to the more general reader who
might be interested primarily in theater history and
theory.

ACKNOWLEDGMENTS

My first and greatest debt is to Robert C. Elliott for
encouragement and criticism in writing the original draft
of this book, for help in its publication, for provocative
ideas on satire, and for his supportive friendship during
hard times. Others who have kindly aided me in pub-
lishing this work are James T. Monroe of the University
of California at Berkeley, Roy Harvey Pearce, David
Crowne, and Leonard Newmark of the University of
California at San Diego, and William McClung at the
University of California Press. I would also like to name
and thank those who have taught me, in person, about
Shakespeare, without suggesting that any of the follow-

ing should be held responsible for my opinions or style: Paul Jorgensen, Remington Paterson, David Robertson, and the late Sigurd Burckhardt.

1: Introduction: A Theory
of Satiric Catharsis

WHETHER AUTHOR or created character, the satirist is distinguished, if not defined,[1] by an urgent desire to see some kind of change in his society. Hatred and censure motivate his emotional invectives or rational attacks on the evils of his time and place. The satirist is more directly concerned with social reform than any other type of literary personage.

But the satirist is distinguished by his speech instead of by his acts. In what way, if at all, does he expect his satiric words to effect societal change? One approach to answering this question would involve us in an analysis of the satiric personality—a knotty business which has already been attempted;[2] or we might become involved in the difficult sociological task of proving empirically the effectiveness of art. I wish to approach the problem, instead, from the point of view of satire's identifying

[1] Robert C. Elliott, "The Definition of *Satire*: A Note on Method," *Yearbook of Comparative and General Literature* (1962), pp. 19–23, sees common to all satire only an elaborate set of "family resemblances" and the factor of attack.

[2] Leonard Feinberg, *The Satirist* (1963), which does, however, contain a thorough bibliography.

1

language and the artistic structures in which it operates.

In a major book on the nature of satire, Robert Elliott explains the power of satiric language in terms of its magical origins.[3] He accounts for the essential nature of sophisticated satire by tracing it to its primitive and archetypal ancestor, the curse. My work is based on an acceptance of this hypothesis about the origin of satire's peculiar forcefulness.

With this anthropological background, I would like to turn to a strictly aesthetic approach to the problem of aesthetic effect. It is productive to transfer Aristotle's suggestion about the cathartic effect of tragedy to drama in which a major character functions as a satirist because the socio-political context of Aristotle's theory (and of Plato's earlier remarks on the subject) perfectly suits the satirist's prime interest in worldly change. Moreover, the emotionally charged nature of satiric language (and of the reactions to it) suggests that some kind of purgation of emotions might be crucial to its stage representation and audience reception. We will want to know: What kind of purgation? With what preconditions? With what variations and what aesthetic effect?

The problem of satiric catharsis divides into two main branches, which tend to become entangled in discussion: the satirist's catharsis and the audience's catharsis. Most commentary on the subject—and there has not been much—deals with the first branch, not my prime interest in this book, but one which should be analyzed before we proceed: that personal, inner catharsis or release felt by the real or fictional satirist when

[3] Robert C. Elliott, *The Power of Satire: Magic, Ritual, Art* (1960), pp. 49–100 especially.

he rails against society. This, evidently, is what Mary
Claire Randolph had in mind when in 1941 she promised
the paper whose title, "A Theory of Satiric Catharsis,"[4]
I have used for Chapter I.

This aspect of satiric purgation goes back to the Roman
verse satirists who, in their various *apologiae*,[5] claimed
a kind of bodily "urge" necessitating their satiric writing. When Horace's *amor scribendi* carries him away
(*rapit*), he is so wrought up that he cannot even sleep
(II, i, 10, 7); he draws his *stilus* ("dagger and pen", line
39), by instinct:

> *ut quo quisque valet suspectos terreat,*
> *utque imperet hoc natura potens, sic collige*
> *mecum: dente lupus, cornu taurus petit; unde,*
> *nisi intus monstratum?*

> (How everyone, using the weapon in which he
> is strong, tries to frighten those whom he fears,
> and how this is at Dame Nature's own com-
> mand, you must infer—as I do—thus: the wolf
> attacks with fangs, the bull with horns—how
> was each taught, if not by instinct?)[6]

and follows his natural compulsion:

> *seu me tranquilla senectus*
> *expectat seu mors atris circumvolat alis,*

[4] Mary Claire Randolph, "The Medical Concept in English
Renaissance Satiric Theory" (1941), p. 157; the paper did not
appear.

[5] Horace, *Sermones* I, iv; I, x; II, i; Persius I and Juvenal I,
discussed in this context by Rogers Lucius Shero, "The Satirist's
Apologia," (1922), pp. 155–159.

[6] *Horace: Satires, Epistles and Ars Poetica*, trans. H. Rushton
Fairclough (1961), p. 131.

> *dives, inops, Romae, seu fors ita iusserit, exsul,*
> *quisquis erit vitae scribam color.*
>
> (lines 57–60)

> (whether peaceful age awaits me, or Death hov-
> ers round with sable wings, rich or poor, in
> Rome, or, if chance so bid, in exile, whatever
> the color of my life, write I must.)

Similarly, when Persius's interlocutor criticizes the satiric
mode, the poet replies that when he looks at the corruption of Rome he *must* speak out; the compulsion rises
from his very innards: *Nolo: quid faciam? sed sum petu-
lanti splene cachinno* (I, 12). ("I would rather not say
it—but what else can I do?—I have a wayward wit and
must have my laugh out.")[7] Juvenal conveys the same
idea in his *difficile est saturam non scribere* (I, 30) where
he expresses his pent-up outrage at the immorality of
the era of Nero and the bad emperors; the overall tone
of the passionate, indignant outburst rhetorically an-
swers his question, *Quid referam quanta siccum iecur
ardeat ira* ("Why tell how my heart burns dry with
rage"[8]): *iecur* is actually the liver, supposedly the seat of
the passions, which for Juvenal demand the satiric outlet.

During the Renaissance this type of personal release
through satire usually was discussed through the medical
metaphors implicit in the term catharsis, while in the
neoclassical period the idea was restated in more abstract

[7] *Juvenal and Persius*, trans. G. G. Ramsay, (1957), p. 317; in
Dryden's translation the compulsion is even more clearly physical:
"I must speak out or burst . . . I cannot rule my spleen; My scorn
rebels and tickles me within."

[8] Ramsay, p. 7; Dryden again stresses the physical: "What indignation boils within my veins."

terms.[9] In 1589 Puttenham observed that though the ancient poets lyricized, they also had to "utter their splenes" (i.e., rail) "or else it seemed their bowels would burst"; when they "got rid of their gall" by "imprecation . . . and cursing" "it was a great easement to the boiling stomacke."[10] Jonson humorously renders the idea of personal satiric release in *Poetaster* (V, i) where he (as "Horace") gives the bad satirist Crispinus (Marston) purgatives to vomit forth the "tumultous heats" of his pent-up satiric words. But we find Pope's version of the traditional idea the simple, "I love to pour out all my self"[11] or, in "Arbuthnot" his gently Horatian version of the sense of natural urgency that made him a satirist:

> *As yet a child, nor yet a fool to fame,*
> *I lisped in numbers, for the numbers came.*
>
> (127–128)

Similarly, Swift felt "born to introduce" his ironic mode,[12] and his hack-writer persona in the Preface to *A Tale of A Tub* feels "a great ease to my conscience" because of what he has written. As learned and sober as Dryden is in his "Discourse Concerning Satire," he nevertheless allows personal revenge as a legitimate motive for satire—thereby implying the right to release passions. Indeed, he even agrees with Heinsius that "The end or scope of satire is to purge the passions"[13] in the way Juvenal and Persius do.

[9] Randolph, p. 135.

[10] George Puttenham, *The Arte of English Poesie*, ed. Edward Arber (1895), pp. 68, 72.

[11] "The First Satire of the Second Book of Horace Imitated (To Mr. Fortescue)," 1.51.

[12] "Verses on the Death of Dr. Swift," 1.57.

[13] *Poetical Works of Dryden*, ed. George R. Noyes (1950), p. 316.

With this sketch of authorial catharsis concluded, we can now turn to the second aspect of satiric catharsis which is the one on which I shall concentrate: the "purifying" psychic release that can occur in the audience beholding a satirist rail upon a stage. This aesthetic mechanism of drama is what Frye refers to when he says, "The principles of catharsis in other fictional forms than tragedy, such as comedy or satire, were not worked out by Aristotle, and have therefore never been worked out since."[14] The key for the application of these principles to satire will be found in the sanative implications and political contexts of Aristotle's use of the term *catharsis*.

Discussing tragedy in the *Poetics* and music in the *Politics*, Aristotle finds a place in his society for at least two kinds of art because of their healthy cathartic effect. Most interpreters agree about the general outline of what he meant by catharsis, even if the details remain debatable.[15] This son to the court physician was suggesting that the performing arts could release certain extreme, and therefore dangerous, emotions that might otherwise prevent citizens from properly fulfilling their daily duties in society. Aesthetic catharsis makes leisure therapeutic and safeguards the state.

This generalization arises first of all from a study of

---

[14] Northrup Frye, *Anatomy of Criticism* (1957), p. 66, but for conjectures about comic catharsis see Lane Cooper, *An Aristotelian Theory of Comedy* (1922), pp. 63–76, 179–182, 224, 228.

[15] Philip Wheelwright, "Catharsis," *Encyclopedia of Poetry and Poetics*, (1965), p. 106, calls his definition only one interpretation among many in a still open debate, but even without considering Aristotle's *Politics* he sees tragic catharsis as a way of preventing what Plato called "anarchy of the soul" through an expressive cure.

the various translations of the controversial definition of catharsis in the *Poetics*. In the Bywater translation, Aristotle stipulates that tragedy must have "incidents arousing pity and fear wherewith to accomplish its catharsis of such emotions."[16] The controversy over the missing definition for the term (Aristotle's *Politics* promised to supply one in the *Poetics*) seems to center around the grammatical ambiguity of the genitive in the word translated as *catharsis of*. Bernays, for example, interprets it to mean the total expulsion of morbid emotions, while Butcher sees it as a clarification or purification of extreme emotions rather than merely an outlet.[17] Most of the major moral, medical, humanitarian, etc.[18] interpretations of the definition are merely variations on this basic argument. Whether or not clarification results in addition to release does not change the basic importance of the medical metaphor and the affectual implications of Aristotle's idea of catharsis.

In his homeopathic interpretation of Aristotle's tragic catharsis in the preface to *Samson Agonistes*, Milton emphasizes the mechanism's resultant tempering and reduction of extreme humors:

[16] *Poetics*, trans. Ingram Bywater (1954), ch. vi, p. 230.

[17] S. H. Butcher, *Aristotle's Theory of Poetry and Fine Art* (1951), p. 255.

[18] Wheelwright, pp. 106–108, notes that Aristotle implied catharsis led to insight and wisdom, while the Italian Renaissance critic Minturno saw delight and profit as its result; Corneille and Racine talked of moral purification, Lessing of an ethical standard of due measure and recognition of fate, Milton of homeopathic cure, Wordsworth of humanitarian elevation and I. A. Richards of resultant reconciliation and equilibrium. Of the major commentators, only Goethe thought Aristotle meant reconciliation among dramatic characters instead of in the spectator.

Tragedy, as it was anciently composed, hath been ever held
the gravest, moralest, and most profitable of all other poems;
therefore said by Aristotle to be of power, by raising pity
and fear, or terror, to purge the mind of those and such like
passions; that is, to temper and reduce them to just measure
with a kind of delight, stirred up by reading or seeing those
passions well imitated. Nor is nature wanting in her own
effects to make good his assertion; for so in physic, things of
melancholic hue and quality are used against melancholy,
sour against sour, salt to remove salt humours.

Whether we talk of Greek wisdom, Renaissance morals
or modern energies, the concept of catharsis generally
implies a tempering in the spectator for a sanative purpose, an essential reduction, even if accompanied by other
aesthetic delights and compensations. In a still controversial study, Gerald F. Else proposes that Aristotle's
catharsis referred to a feature of the structure of tragedy
rather than an emotional end-effect on the spectator.[19]
Else does have Goethe on his side of the controversy,
but as appealing as his argument sounds, at its conclusion even Else admits that his entire interpretation of
catharsis in the *Poetics* cannot be reconciled with the allusion to catharsis in *Politics VIII*.

Here in a political context Aristotle uses the homeopathic idea of catharsis which Plato mentioned (in the
Laws) in respect to music as a cure for religious frenzy.
Aristotle describes the proper education for the ruling
class in an ideal state; all elements of this education must
contribute to good citizenship and stable government.

---

[19] Gerald F. Else, *Aristotle's Poetics: The Argument* (1963), pp.
423–447; Else would restrict the "much-inflated" term to a comment on the tragic plot (catharsis as the result, through *anagnor-
isis*, of *hamartia*).

Because leisure must be properly used in the healthy state in order to maintain contented citizens, he here suggests the therapeutic use of various types of music. We must use the most ethical harmonies for education

and the active and passionate kinds for listening to when others are performing (for any experience that occurs violently in some souls is found in all, though with different degrees of intensity—for example pity and fear, and also religious excitement; for some persons are very liable to this form of emotion, and under the influence of sacred music we see these people, when they use tunes that violently arouse the soul, being thrown into a state as if they had received medicinal treatment and taken a purge; the same experience then must come also to the compassionate and the timid and the other emotional people generally in such degree as befalls each individual of these classes, and all must undergo a purgation and a pleasant feeling of relief; and similarly also the purgative melodies afford harmless delight to people).[20]

Aristotle can accept variations in art because he sees sanative, political uses for each type when properly analyzed and accurately applied.

This application of the theory of purgation to music suggests that Aristotle thought of catharsis as a principle of art rather than merely an aspect of tragedy. F. L. Lucas conjectures that Aristotle believed epic and lyric poetry had a similar, if milder, cathartic effect, "while comedy might release and relieve other emotions such as aggressiveness, malice or licentiousness";[21] in this

[20] *Aristotle: Politics*, trans. H. Rackham (1959), VIII, 7, 1342a, p. 671.

[21] Frank L. Lucas, *Literature and Psychology* (1951), pp. 274–275; it must be noted that Lucas calls this conjecture ingenious and beside the point, defending the theater as "not merely a matter of intoxication but also of experience."

light, he continues, "literature becomes a device for re-establishing that happy mean which Aristotle found the basis of the virtues." Assuming, then, that Aristotle's theory could be applied to satiric drama as well, we must now complete the analogy with the pity and fear of tragedy.

I am defining satiric drama as that type of play in which a major character functions as a satirist, his identifying language marked by habitual curse, invective, or critical railing. In the interpretation of Aristotle which I have accepted, the spectator's fear must derive from a sympathetic experiencing of the hero's fear in his tragic entanglement. As the tragic hero is characterized by this *fear*, so the satirist in the play is characterized by his *hatred*, for this is his basic reaction to the world order facing him, and the spectator must share this hatred. Butcher rightly concludes that fear is the primary emotion from which pity derives its meaning,[22] because the tragic spectator will surely pity the hero whose fear he shares. To carry through the analogy (fear: pity = hatred: censure), then, the spectator of a satiric drama will *censure* while the tragic spectator pities; and, while tragedy elicits emotions in response to the fated or divinely ordained disorder of life, satire does so in response to the societal or man-made disorder of life.

Pure satiric drama, then, should raise emotions of hatred in the spectator who attends to the satirist character's expression of contempt; the audience will tend to be dangerously incited to radical criticism, to the censure of its society, to the desire to change the temporal order.

[22] Butcher, p. 257, working from an examination of Aristotle's *Rhetoric*.

Yet if a satiric catharsis operates, the play's action will purge the audience of these disturbing emotions and impulses, just as tragedy purges its audience of the impulse to contend with the divine order after the play is over.

Whether or not such a satiric catharsis takes place "in general" is as impossible to decide as whether Aristotle or Plato was right about the function of art in society. Plato did not invoke the dual traditions[23] of medical and religious purification through catharsis to redeem art as a nonsubversive societal element. In the *Republic* Socrates claims that the imitation of low beings, which is the mainstay of much dramatic poetry, would be demeaning for both rulers and citizens; when a poetic genius enters the state, he says,

we shall bow down before a being with such miraculous powers of giving pleasure; but we shall tell him that we are not allowed to have any such person in our commonwealth; we shall crown him with fillets of wool, anoint his head with myrrh, and conduct him to the borders of some other country.[24]

Later, he again takes up the subject—in terms which clearly prompted Aristotle's brilliant answer in the *Poetics*. Socrates says that most dramatic poetry, whether tragic or comic, is reprehensible because it appeals to the lowly emotions instead of the lofty reasoning powers (Book X, 602–605). Furthermore, it corrupts character by encouraging the sympathetic indulgence of emotions. Pity and admiration released at a drama will prompt their release in real-life situations, undermining reason and restraint as societal forces: watching a clown will make one act the buffoon;

[23] Wheelwright, p. 107.
[24] *The Republic*, trans. F. M. Cornford (1964), p. 85.

similar effects are produced by poetic representation of love
and anger and all those desires and feelings of pleasure or pain
which accompany our every action. It waters the growth of
passions which should be allowed to wither away and sets
them up in control, although the goodness and happiness of
our lives depend on their being held in subjection.[25]

It is only when we examine individual satiric dramas
that we can decide whether Aristotle or Plato was right,
in that particular instance, about what art does to us.
And even then, as literary critics instead of experimental
psychologists, or sociologists, we are necessarily involved
in conjectures about aesthetic effect inferred from our
understanding of dramatic form. We will be concerned,
then, with how the author manipulates the satirist in his
dual function as character involved in a fictional plot and
as critic of a representative society. If the author who has
created a satirist effects a satiric catharsis in the audience
—a purging of the "change" emotions of hatred and censure—he will carry out Aristotle's theory of art but his
satire will defeat its own implied purpose of changing
society; if he prevents catharsis he will realize Plato's
view of art by profoundly disturbing his society.

To what sort of texts might we now turn for illustration
of this theory? I have been discussing it in terms of the
stage drama because that is the most familiar application
of catharsis from the time of the *Poetics,* and because
that is my primary interest. However, as we know, the
word also has been applied even to nonliterary forms of
art. We might venture, then, to look for satiric catharsis
in nondramatic forms. Indeed, with the help of modern

[25] *Republic,* pp. 338–339.

persona criticism we could keep in mind the Aristotelian tragedy model while looking at the treatment of the satirist character in, say, Pope's "Epistle to Dr. Arbuthnot." However, in the traditional formal verse satire we cannot really discuss catharsis with its full dramatic complications because of the incompleteness of the mimetic structure. The author is closely connected to his satirist persona whose self-purgation (our first branch of catharsis) becomes the main focus of the work. In order to speak forcefully he must assume that when he has purged himself of the vile words building up inside him, he will have destroyed (by exposure) society's vileness. The interlocutor affords too scant a vehicle for audience identification to permit that mimetic credibility which is the first prerequisite for any kind of dramatic catharsis.

Turning to the stage again, we should not be surprised to find that Shakespeare creates a range of great satirists as well as tragic heroes, clowns, romantics, and warriors. Indeed, many of these character categories are intermixed in the satirist. Living at a time when satire was very much alive (Hall, Marston, Jonson, Nash, Rowlands), although not as sophisticated as it was to become a century later, Shakespeare had the opportunity to incorporate the satiric tradition, as easily as any other, into his highly synthetic work. Nevertheless, his satire has been discussed much less frequently than other aspects of his canon, and in the major criticism satiric catharsis is indirectly alluded to only by C. L. Barber[26] in respect to the "release" in the Falstaff plays. O. J. Campbell's provocative explanation of the form of *Troilus and Cres-*

[26] Cesar Lombardi Barber, *Shakespeare's Festive Comedy* (1959), ch. VIII.

sida in his *Comicall Satyre*[27] has given scholars good
reason to look at that play as something rare in satiric
drama (see Chapter V); his *Shakespeare's Satire*[28] is less
influential because it discusses so many different kinds
of undefined and vaguely satirical commentary in the
plays.

I find that Shakespeare invents five full-fledged primary satirists: Margaret d'Anjou in the *Henry VI-Richard
III* tetralogy, Falstaff in the *Henry IV* plays, Jaques in *As
You Like It*, Thersites in *Troilus and Cressida* and Apemantus in *Timon of Athens* (with Timon as the important
secondary satirist). I identify these as satirists by the particular kind of language they persistently use: railing,
invective and castigation, or the actual curse language
from which these derive. (Others, such as Hamlet, use
the satiric mode of speaking at times, but they do not
found their whole identities on it and influence their plays
as satirists; Caliban is certainly a satiric curser, but he
is kept to a subsidiary role in *The Tempest*.) It is as if
the main personae of formal verse satires have been set
into fully developed mimetic worlds. Here the first important "society" available for purgation and purification is
that within the play's world. Our problem of satiric
catharsis thus divides into two questions: How does the
hating, censuring satirist character affect the play's world?
and then, How does that depicted world affect the audience's emotions of hatred and censure? To answer the
first we must analyze each text to decide what kind of a
disruption the satirist causes within the play and how he

[27] Oscar James Campbell, *Comicall Satyre and Shakespeare's
Troilus and Cressida* (1938), passim.
[28] Oscar James Campbell, *Shakespeare's Satire* (1943).

affects the dramatic resolution. For the second, we must infer the appropriate audience reaction to each variation of satiric drama.

Chapter II deals with Shakespeare's first historical tetralogy, in which Margaret d'Anjou persistently speaks a primitive sort of satire—the plain curse. In her long conflict with the Yorkists she suffers defeat, but her powerful curse falls heavily upon Richard III in the final play of the group, the structure of which we will examine. Her words alone fail to purge the play's world of evil, except in the indirect, perhaps still magical, sense. To the audience she offers a partial outlet for the rejection and censure of the evil Richard, and her function as a societal "complainer" emphasizes the very controversial nature of the history plays, revolving as they do upon "just" and "unjust" claims to power. But we end up rejecting the satirist along with her victim: satiric catharsis coincides with the multiplicity of evil and "fault" in Shakespeare's interpretation of the whole bloody pageant of the War of the Roses.

In *Henry IV* (Chapter III) Shakespeare shows a much more refined interest in satiric technique. Here Falstaff is the skillful satirist dealing in witty invective and word play rather than plain curse. Just as Margaret trained Elizabeth into the satiric mode, so Falstaff taps Hal's latent satiric talents and moralistic inclinations. The prince rejects the low satirist who, if portrayed as a comic figure, purges the play's censorious emotions (e.g., mockery of justice and honor) in his role as misrule scapegoat, leaving the audience unprovoked. If romanticized, Falstaff becomes the tragical scapegoat (from tragedy as "goat song") but without the accompanying catharsis of high

tragedy resulting from noble suffering; result: the play
as a whole disturbs the audience and the satire "works."

In *As You Like It* (Chapter IV) Shakespeare avoids this
ambiguity of portrayal by employing a clear-cut fool-
scapegoat who is soundly rejected in the play's structure
and thereby purges Arden of discordant emotions. Jaques
becomes the purgative cure for the fictional society. A
kind of comical-satiric catharsis results in which the audience is purged of its debilitating tendency to find everything in life ridiculous. Shakespeare prevents his railer,
Jaques, from forming a Platonic-type of art which disturbs its audience; the author prevents his satire from
working.

By about the year 1602 Shakespeare was finally ready
to write a "comicall satyre" that will work in the aesthetic
sense of disturbing his audience to the core. Chapter V
deals with *Troilus and Cressida*, in which the most vile
and disease-minded of Shakespeare's satirists, Thersites,
infects the entire play with his caustic views. No tragic
or comic resolution is possible because the satirist character controls the action. No satiric catharsis occurs because he transmits his "disease" to other characters rather
than purging himself of it. The energies of social disturbance flow from the play's fictional world to the real
waning world of Elizabeth's last years. This is the kind
of art Plato feared.

Timon (Chapter VI) provides the exact inversion of
this aesthetic mechanism. Here there is a full cathartic
circle in operation: Shakespeare, on the border between
the play's world and the real world, creates satirist Apemantus whose critical forces within the play in turn convert Timon into a raging satirist. The misanthrope hero

rises to tragic proportions and his death effects a catharsis of such emotions of social censure that would have rocked the real world of 1609. He becomes the tragic scapegoat that the prime satirist (Apemantus) cannot become by virtue of his ties with the Vice character of early comedy.

Shakespeare's chronological development of the satiric persona shows a movement from the most primitive aspects of the satirist's function in society to the most sophisticated, a development analogous to the development of Old Comedy to New, of medieval raillery to the satire of the Enlightenment. After investigating the possible uses of the dramatized satirist in a play, Shakespeare, at the height of his powers, is able to effect or prevent a satiric catharsis—a purging of the "change emotions"— according to his inclination.

The satirist's destructive powers have long been acknowledged;[29] the theory of satiric catharsis illuminates his sanative powers. The authorial satirist can work toward curing the actual world by preventing catharsis in his play, or he can effect a mimetic cure by causing catharsis.

In the first case the societal cure appears as somatic disturbance—just as the satirist-physician's remedy first aggravates the sore spot. There is ample evidence in satiric literature, especially of the Renaissance, that the satirist considers himself physician to his society,[30] that

[29] Randolph, p. 142, lists a page of destructive terms for Renaissance satire, and on a wider level, see Elliott, *Power of Satire*, chs. I and II, and his Appendix on The Curse.

[30] Randolph, p. 143, notes, e.g., that Horace praised Lucilius for "rubbing the city down with much salt" and for "peeling the skins off hypocrites" and Persius praised Lucilius for having "flayed the city." In his free translation of *Das Narren Schiff* (1509) Alex.

he sets out to purge it of what he diagnoses as moral ill through the bitter medicines of his stinging wit and harsh invective. The rare drama that maintains that stasis of plot[31] which prevents traditional dramatic resolution, and also features a satirist to make the social criticism explicit, will cause a disturbance in the audience as a body. It is strong medicine. Only then can the audience, as a part of the body politic, be expected to act in response to art.

Most public censure enunciated by stage satirists results only in mimetic cure. This usually necessitates the expulsion or rejection of the satirist who represents all discordant elements in the play's world. Through some variety of the Scapegoat mechanism the dramatist resolves the conflicts of his play's world. The audience gets rid of its emotion by "blowing off steam," as Freud said,[32] along with the satirist, and then turns against him to

---

Barclay sets out "to clense the vanyte and madness of folysshe people of whom over great nombre is in the Royalme of Englande." And when Thom. Drant rendered Horace's satires he used the title, "A MEDICINABLE/ Morall, that is, the two Bookes of Horace Satyres. . . ."

[31] Alvin Kernan, *The Cankered Muse* (1959), p. 31, considers the "normal satiric plot" in general to be characterized by a "stasis" which is reconsidered as a "curling in upon itself" in his *Plot of Satire* (1965), p. 100.

[32] "Psychopathic Characters on the Stage," *Standard Edition of the Complete Psychological Works of Sigmund Freud*, trans. James Strachey et al., vol. VII (1962), p. 305; the special preconditions for this release are delineated in *Jokes and Their Relation to the Unconscious: Standard Edition*, vol. VIII (1962), pp. 150–158; since Freud also discusses the discharge response to tragedy and to the "uncanny," Norman Holland, *Psychoanalysis and Shakespeare* (1966), p. 36 ff, feels justified in applying the release theory for jokes to literature in general.

enjoy participating in the serene unreality of a world which has banished its moral gadflies.

Our inquiry into the worlds of Shakespeare's five major satirists, then, will revolve around the controversy between the Marxist and Freudian view of art. The conflict has been described as follows:

> Most anthropologists and many Marxists . . . believe that art is and should be a tool of society; that its function is to create or tighten solidarity within a social group or to maintain or bring about a particular form of society; that, in fact, if art is living and vital it always tends and should tend to some outcome in social action and that if it does not do so it is sterile.
>
> The Freudians, on the other hand, building partly upon Schiller's "play" theory, see art as the adult's version of childish pretense-playing, a form of wish-fulfillment related to dreams and to fantasy or daydreams.[33]

Before we can say what art "*should* tend to" (action or therapy), we must find out what a representative range of it *does* tend to—which is the purpose of the next five chapters.

[33] Elisabeth Schneider, *Aesthetic Motive* (1939), pp. 2–3.

2: The Satiric Curser
Against Richard III

BECAUSE MARGARET OF ANJOU is the only character to appear in all of Shakespeare's first set of history plays, she serves to unify the tetralogy. She may have been put in at the very end of *1 Henry VI* only when the four plays were assembled for consecutive performance, but she figures more and more actively in each part until *Richard III* where she assumes her final role as anathema to the Yorkists and satiric-curser of the immoral king.

Since to my knowledge it has not been observed that Margaret functions as a satirist, even by O. J. Campbell in his wide-ranging *Shakespeare's Satire*, I will present the evidence for this view from the three parts of *Henry VI* before analyzing the structure of *Richard III*. We must determine how the old satirist Queen Margaret affects that play's internal world and then return to the question of satiric catharsis to ask: How does the satiric element within the play affect the audience's emotions of hatred and censure in the external world?

I

We now believe that satiric language stems from curse language, whose power depends on the preternatural

force of magical verses uttered by certain extraordinary
individuals; usually poets, these primitive satirists might
practice magical rites, but they depended on the inherent
power of their invectives, their mocking or riddling
verses, and their specially concatenated words, rhymes,
and rhythms.[1] As it happens Shakespeare's first set of history plays opens with an overt reference to magical
verses:[2]

> *Henry is dead and never shall revive . . .*
> *What? Shall we curse the planets of mishap*
> *That Plotted thus our glory's overthrow?*
> *Or shall we think the subtile-witted French*
> *Conjurers and sorcerers, that, afraid of him,*
> *By magical verses have contrived his end?*
>
> (I,i,18, 23–27)

Thus from the very outset the French, countrymen of
Margaret d'Anjou, are identified with the magical power
of poetry to inflict harm.

Indeed the bulk of *1 Henry VI* concerns, not Margaret,
who only appears at the end, but the powerful Joan La
Pucelle who curses like a witch, but whom the French
call a saint. Joan's every word and act challenge English
power; an aura of witchery and magic surrounds her.
Another sharp-tongued female, the Countess of Au-
vergne, adds a further French threat in II, iii where she

---

[1] Robert C. Elliott, *The Power of Satire* (1960), p. 50.

[2] James G. Rice, "Shakespeare's Curse: Relation to Elizabethan
Curse Tradition and Drama" (1947), p. 157, calls this the only
certain reference to magical verses in Shakespeare, but, as Elliott
notes, p. 35, Rosalynd refers to rat-rhyming in *AYLI*, III, ii, 186. All
quotations from Shakespeare refer to George Lyman Kittredge, ed.,
Complete Works of Shakespeare (1936).

attempts to outwit and capture the English hero Talbot.[3]
When Margaret finally appears in this staging of English
history she must be seen in the context of the national
associations built up by the countess and Joan.

The young Margaret of *1 Henry VI*, V, iii, is quite
consistent[4] with the proud, strong, sharp-tongued trou-
ble-maker of the next three plays; the character is merely
underplayed to suit the youth and beauty which still
operate in her favor and make unnecessary for the present rash actions or rash words. Earlier in the scene Joan
has failed in her last-ditch effort to get supernatural support for her cause: the fiends she conjures refuse to help
her. By the time she exits cursing, "A plaguing mischief
light on Charles and thee!" (39), she has identified herself as a laughable, because impotent, witch. Margaret
then enters with new "charms" to replace those of La
Pucelle.

Though a prisoner, Margaret's first words are haughty:[5] "Margaret my name, and daughter to a king, The
King of Naples, whosoe'er thou art." Suffolk immediately
falls victim to her charms and finds his very speech con-
founded (line 71). She then shows her talent for ridicule
when she calls him a carpenter (line 90) though she

---

[3] Sigurd Burckhardt, *Shakespearean Meanings* (1968), pp. 47–77,
focuses on this episode in his explication of the play's peculiar
"vaunt-taunt" style.

[4] An examination of her language in this scene disproves the
view of her as a Cordelia-like damsel-princess suddenly converted
to a scourge in the next play—an idea offered by Thomas H. Mc-
Neal, "Margaret of Anjou: Romantic Princess and Troubled
Queen" (1958), pp. 1–10.

[5] Burckhardt, pp. 52–53, finds Margaret here "contentious rather than content, overbearing rather than humble" and the em-
bodiment of the play's vaunt-taunt style.

knows him an earl. Within a few moments (about 100 lines) she contrives to change from the powerless female captive to mistress and queen as an enamoured Suffolk promises to marry her to Henry VI. The end of this scene, like its beginning, includes the curses of Joan La Pucelle. It is fitting that after Margaret's entry into England is assured, Joan puts her curse on the country by wishing it "darkness, and the gloomy shade of death" (V, iv, 89); for Margaret will plague the country.

In *2 Henry VI* Margaret envies and fears a rival to the throne to such an extent that she becomes "England's bloody scourge." In this still presatirist phase her character develops toward the "traditionally vengeful and ill-natured"[6] personality of the satirist (though she does not assume full satiric function until *Richard III*). Ten years pass during the course of *2 Henry VI*. Margaret appears in all acts, in ten out of twenty-four scenes, dallying with magical verses, but always finally opposing her enemies with physical force rather than satire. Magic is important in this play: Hume deals with witches and conjurors on behalf of Eleanor, Duchess of Gloucester, and the prophecies of the witch Margery Jourdain come true. But Margaret continues to avoid affiliation with such culpable magic as outright conjuring and witchery while she whets her verbal wit for the finer magic of the satiric curse.

Her first speech (I, i, 24 ff) is hailed as being skillful: Henry sees grace and wisdom in his new queen. But old Gloucester knows better when he calls the marriage

[6] Mary Claire Randolph. "Celtic Smiths and Satirists: Partners in Sorcery" (1941), p. 195.

"fatal" for Margaret herself is England's curse. Her first act as queen is to rip up a petition and cry, "Away, base cullions!" (I, iii, 43). Unwarranted envy and desire for vengeance motivate her fierce anger against the Duchess of Gloucester; the scene (I, iii, 142 ff) in which Margaret boxes Eleanor's ears—almost low comedy—comes from the medieval tradition and warns us that this queen's rhetorical powers may find their true function in a mode not strictly tragical.

We are considering a point in literature at which the magical curse and magical satire are still extremely difficult to differentiate, especially since belief in magic was transitional and equivocal during the Renaissance. Inasmuch as Margaret speaks in verse instead of prose and indulges in ridicule we may think of her as a satirist, but at this point, since we are concerned with character,

perhaps the best approach is to look at both curse and satire as relatively undifferentiated responses to the threats and the possibilities of a hostile environment. Behind them both is the will to attack, to do harm, to kill—in some negative way to control one's world.[7]

Margaret's destruction of her self-declared enemies, Protector Humphrey Duke of Gloucester and his wife Eleanor, is a case in point. While the actual *harm* comes about through her nonmagical royal power, the *attack* depends on her verbal power and is marked by references to the primitive magic of incantational Celtic verse.

Act III, scene i, opens with Margaret's harsh offensive against poor Humphrey whom we have just seen contrite and good in his undeserved misery. Here her words are

[7] Elliott, *Power of Satire*, p. 292.

persuasive and critical, aimed to destroy, but unsatiric, even in the widest sense, because unmarked by signs of either magical rhetoric or the traditional forms of railing or invective. But when Henry remains unconvinced of Gloucester's guilt, even by Suffolk's maxims (lines 51–55), Margaret launches into the curse technique of animal name-calling which tries to identify the victim with a lower order of life with traditionally bad connotations:

> *Seems he a dove? His feathers are but borrowed,*
> *For he's disposed as the hateful raven.*
> *Is he a lamb? His skin is surely lent him,*
> *For he's inclined as is the ravenous wolf.*

> (75–79)

Accused of treason, Humphrey protests against the plotters, especially Margaret who he knows has "laid disgraces" on his head and "stirred up" the king against him. When he excitedly breaks out of his usual mode of speech, his "railing" is found "intolerable," his rage, proof of treason, and his "twitting" of Margaret "with ignominious words, though clerkly couched," dangerous. Against the king's better conscience Humphrey is convicted because he has risked satiric speech but lacks that satiric gift which Margaret is just beginning to use to accomplish her ambitions.

In all of this Margaret seems motivated by personal hatred to effect the painful downfall of her enemies and thereby satisfy a private rage with which we have little sympathy.[8] Yet the scene of Gloucester's fall was pre-

---

[8] In the English tradition cursing is condoned when "love of public justice" motivates it instead of "personal hate"; cf. Rice, p. 42. Satirists traditionally make the claim to defend public justice.

ceded by a labored, reasoned exposition of the Yorkist
claim to the throne (II, ii) and is concluded with York's
decision to stir up the rebels in Ireland to unseat the king.
Henry is characterized as noble, worthy, sensitive, reasonable, and a good judge of character; he is willing to
do what is best for England and becomes an active, strong
king when he realizes the meaning of Gloucester's death
and banishes Suffolk. Thus, as morally unattractive as
Margaret appears with her private rage, she also functions as a kind of public curser (she curses outright in
III, ii) who has some social sanction because she serves
"to promote, through negative means, the welfare of a
particular group"[9]—here the Lancastrians. But until she
becomes the full satiric-curser of *Richard III*, the morality of her verbal thrusts will be kept ambiguous. The
satirist's position is defined only against the existence
of an absolute, immoral (as defined by the satirist) status
quo; a state of protracted civil war undermines the satiric
target.

A satirist has to be—or pretend to be—an underdog
of some kind. Perhaps that is why satirizing in the primitive sense of the malediction makes its major appearance
in this play when Henry banishes Suffolk, Margaret's
lover. She curses Henry and Warwick:

> *Mischance and sorrow go along with you!*
> *Heart's discontent and sour affliction*
> *Be playfellows to keep you company!*
> *There's two of you; the devil make a third,*
> *And threeforld vengeance tend upon your steps!*
>
> (III, ii, 300–304)

[9] Elliott, *Power of Satire*, p. 286, referring to the public curser
in general.

When she challenges Suffolk to curse his enemy, he begins by mocking cursers and their magic:

A plague upon them! Wherefore should I curse them?
Would curses kill as doth the mandrake's groan,
I would invent as bitter searching terms,
As curst, as harsh, and horrible to hear,
Delivered strongly through my fixed teeth,
With full as many signs of deadly hate,
As lean-faced Envy in her loathsome cave.
My tongue should stumble in mine earnest words,
Mine eyes should sparkle like the beaten flint,
Mine hair be fixed an end, as one distract;
Ay, every joint should seem to curse and ban;

(309–319)

but he then launches into the real thing[10] purely for its
personally cathartic effect:

And even now my burthened heart would break
Should I not curse them. Poison be their drink!
Gall, worse than gall, the daintiest that they taste!
Their sweetest shade a grove of cypress trees!
Their chiefest prospect murdering basilisks!
Their softest touch as smart as lizards' stings!
Their music frightful as the serpent's hiss,
And boding screech owls make the consort full!
All the foul terrors in dark-seated hell—

(320–328)

As if aware that their cause is not fully just or untainted
enough to risk satire, Margaret warns him to stop "lest

---

[10] Mary Claire Randolph, "The Neo-Classical Theory of the
Formal Verse Satire" (1939), quoted by Rice, p. 222, as a malediction in the Celtic manner; Rice, p. 224, characterizes it as having
the thoroughness of the medieval anathema plus Senecan imagery.

these dread curses . . . recoil"[11] on the speaker. Indeed
throughout the rest of the play she hardens herself in
adversity and sallies forth to the battlefield for revenge
rather than risk her bloodied lips in the dangerous business of the satiric curse.

In *3 Henry VI*, although Margaret shows the disposition of the satirist, she is still too much the "femme
d'action . . . à se preoccuper d'interventions surnatu-
relle."[12] In the first act her anger at the promised dis-
inheritance of her son becomes the major force that un-
does the truce Henry has just concluded. She vents her
anger by calling Henry a "timorous wretch" (I, i, 231)
and goes off to lead an army against Richard Plantagenet,
Duke of York, and his sons. When her men capture the
duke (I, iv) she acknowledges her hate and mocks him
with a paper crown. As with Humphrey in Part 2, her
presence causes a reasonable man to rail: he calls her
"she-wolf of France," "tiger's heart wrapped in a woman's hide" and curses her to misery. She bloodily kills
him and contemptuously sends his head to York. In act
II this "proud insulting Queen" (i, 168) calls Warwick
a coward and lashes out at Richard Crookback who replies in kind in his "Iron of Naples" speech (II, ii, 139 ff)
—a preview of the next play. She depends on her verbal

---

[11] Elliott, *Power of Satire*, p. 291, notes, "Both satire and curse
may be lethal, whether they accord with justice or not; but a
tradition exists that the unjust satire and the unjust curse will
recoil onto him who utters them." According to St. Paul, God said,
"Vengeance is mine" and forbade cursing; St. Thomas condones
cursing only when it conforms with the will of God (Rice, p. 42).

[12] Paul Reyher, *Essai Sur les Idées dans l'oeuvre de Shakespeare*
(1947), p. 238.

skills to argue her cause at the court of Louis XI, but by
V, iv, she is once again leading her soldiers into battle.

Margaret makes her final transition from doer to speaker, from fighter to satirist, between V, iv and the next
scene where she is taken prisoner. To cheer her con-
stituents in V, iv she gives a long strained speech in
the high style (unsuited to her) complete with the hack-
neyed simile of the ship of state. It falls quite flat; she is
soon to be defeated in physical battle for the last time.
In the next scene she is the prisoner of Edward IV
who, with his brothers, Clarence and Richard, stabs
her son to death for "railing" too much like his mother
(line 38). The moralistic boy had hit the three brothers'
weaknesses:

> *Lascivious Edward, and thou perjured George,*
> *And thou misshapen Dick, I tell ye all,*
> *I am your better.*

Richard wants to kill Margaret too lest she "live to
fill the world with words" (line 44), but his brother says
no. She vents her sorrow over her son's death and calls
the Yorks "Butchers and villains, bloody cannibals" (line
61). And she exits with the curse which Richard will
fulfill in the next play, "So come to you and yours as to
this prince!"

II

As we have seen, in the *Henry VI* plays Margaret was
set up as a primitive satirist by virtue of (1) her affiliation
with magic, (2) her skillful use of language, especially
ridicule and curse, (3) her tendency to make cursers or

railers out of interlocutors, (4) her growing personality of discontent, manifested in envy, hatred and censure, even to the point of (5) our partial rejection[13] of her. Only in *Richard III*, however, is she finally in a position to devote herself to satire; only when she relinquishes powerful *action* can she infuse full power into her *speech*.

Margaret fulfills almost all of the conditions James Rice cites (pp. 7–15) for the effective magical curser: she is politically *impotent*;[14] yet she still has the *authority* of a one-time Queen of England; and she is *old*. (The other condition, of being *parent* to the one cursed, she transfers during the course of the play to the Duchess of York.) Margaret marshals against Richard the linguistic forces of the play's wronged women who hurl maledictions at him. In a sense, as A. P. Rossiter says (p. 13), the play's protagonists are "the personality of Richard and the curse of Margaret," which in Tudor history stood for an aspect of "retributive justice"; Margaret is the "living ghost of Lancaster." In her associations with dead royalty and magical language Margaret transmits that supernatural force which L. B. Campbell says Shakespeare used "to enhance the horror of the play and to contribute to the impression of a divine vengeance meting out punishment for sin."[15] (In the last part of this chapter I will

[13] Rejection develops into what Elliott calls the theme of the satirist-satirized, which I pursue below in section III in relation to the cathartic mechanism of satiric drama.

[14] As Arthur Percival Rossiter, *Angel With Horns* (1961), p. 14, puts it: she is "the last stage or age of woman-in-politics: she who has been beautiful, fiercely passionate, queenly, dominating, master of armies, *generalissima*; now old, defeated, empty of everything but fierce bitterness, the illimitable bitterness and rancour of political zeal."

[15] Lily Bess Campbell, *Shakespeare's Histories: Mirrors of Elizabethan Policy* (1958), p. 317.

consider the ethical complications arising from the past immorality of such avengers as Margaret.)

Her curses structure the play. In I, iii she pronounces the magic curses which Rivers and Grey recall at III, iii, and which are fulfilled in V, iii. But the victims must also curse themselves before her curses work. In I, ii Anne curses the future wife of Richard; in IV, i she meets her own curse. Buckingham meets his own curse of act II in V, i. And Richard, under pressure of Elizabeth in IV, iv, curses himself to the fate he encounters at the end, which coincides with Margaret's earlier curse against him. As we will see, by prevailing upon the women in the famous lamentation scene (IV, iv), Margaret indirectly effects Richard's downfall.

In the wooing of Anne (I, ii) Richard must overcome the curse language before he can conquer the woman. Anne, with good cause, hates him and censures his actions in the language of vituperation and invective. She names him as the devil; she calls upon God, Heaven and Earth to avenge Richard's slaughter of her family. But in this play, "Prayers that are offered as curses by those with hatred in their hearts are answered by a divine justice without pity."[16] Anne cursed herself when she cursed Richard's future wife; she must then be sacrificed as God's instrument to achieve justice. Although she knows better, she eventually succumbs to Richard's Christian plea to render good for bad, blessings for curses, and to his devilish flattery of her. And in the midst of their encounter, Anne cites Queen Margaret's eye-witness testimony as the unfailing proof of Richard's guilt at Tewkesbury. Margaret is thus introduced before her

[16] L. B. Campbell, p. 317, who thinks the play's God must be that of the Old Testament; cf. Rice, p. 204.

appearance in the next scene: her function will be to
expose and then to oppose unto death the evil Richard.

Before Margaret enters the great cursing scene (I, iii),
Queen Elizabeth, wife to the ailing Edward IV, is shown
exasperated with the open contempt Richard has shown
for her by his "blunt upbraiding," "bitter scoffs" and
"gross taunts." Although old Margaret vents her bitter
jealousy of Elizabeth even as she enters, her dramatic
mission is emphasized as she hovers about the background making choric asides which undercut Richard's
deceitful exposition at every point. He presumes to tell
Elizabeth, "my pains are quite forgot." Margaret speaks
aside:

> *Out, devil! I do remember them too well.*
> *Thou kill'dst my husband Henry in the Tower.*
> *And Edward, my poor son, at Tewksbury.*
>
> (117–120)

He: "To royalize his [Edward IV's] blood I spent my
own." She (aside): "Ay, and much better blood than his
or thine." When her imperious nature can no longer stay
out of the dispute she advances calling for everyone to
tremble and bow before her. As wild as it is, in performance the speech must not be allowed to tip into the
ludicrous: Richard must really recoil when he cries, "Foul
wrinkled witch, what makest thou in my sight?" because he truly fears the supernatural and Margaret has
come like a ghost out of banishment with her quasi-
magical satire-curse. As W. Clemen says, this scene's
gloomy effect depends on "Margaret's power to curse
and to utter abusive and threatening imprecations, a
power against which not even Richard can stand up."[17]

17 Wolfgang H. Clemen, "Anticipation and Foreboding in Shakespeare's Early Histories" (1953), p. 27.

But he fights curse with curse by reminding her of his father's dying curse on her for her cruelty in taunting him and killing young Rutland. But in this world of perpetual historical revenge, the tyrant of one decade becomes the tyrannized in the next. Hearing York's curse again only reminds Margaret of her losses and enrages her.

> *Can curses pierce the clouds and enter heaven?*
> *Why then, give way, dull clouds, to my quick curses!*
>
> (195–196)

Through the optative mood in lines whose symmetry embodies the idea of vengeance, she then forecasts the play's plot. For King Edward she picks up where her son left off in the previous play: "Though not by war, by surfeit die your king!" For the heir to the Yorkist throne:

> *Edward thy son, that now is Prince of Wales,*
> *For Edward our son, that was Prince of Wales,*
> *Die in his youth by like untimely violence!*
>
> (199–201)

For Elizabeth:

> *Thyself a queen, for me that was a queen,*
> *Outlive thy glory, like my wretched self!*
>
> (202–203)

And the followers Rivers, Dorset and Hastings are cursed to die by accident.

All these evidently take their curses in awed silence, but Richard cries out against Margaret's power: "Have done thy charm, thou hateful withered hag!" She replies with her incantational chef d'oeuvre:

And leave out thee? Stay, dog, for thou shalt hear me.
If heaven have any grievous plague in store
Exceeding those that I can wish upon thee,
O let them keep it till thy sins be ripe,
And then hurl down their indignation
On thee, the troubler of the poor world's peace!
The worm of conscience still begnaw thy soul!
Thy friend suspect for traitors while thou livest,
And take deep traitors for thy dearest friends!
No sleep close up that deadly eye of thine,
Unless it be while some tormenting dream
Affrights thee with a hell of ugly devils!
Thou elvish-mark'd, abortive, rooting hog!
Thou that wast seal'd in thy nativity
The slave of nature and the son of hell!
Thou slander of thy heavy mother's womb!
Thou loathed issue of thy father's loins!
Thou rag of honour! thou detested—

(216–233)

But Richard, knowing the rules of cursing, interrupts: at the crucial pronunciation of the name which mysteriously traps the named in magical bonds,[18] he trickily puts in "Margaret!" before she can say her "Richard!" She cries, "O! let me make the period to my curse!" Elizabeth warns the old woman that she has cursed herself, but such trickery cannot stop her. Before she leaves

---

[18] Elliott, *Power of Satire*, p. 39, cites the following Celtic satire to illustrate the power of naming:

> Evil, death, short life to Caier!
> Let spears of battle wound him, Caier!
> Caier . . .! Caier . . .! Caier under earth,
> Under ramparts, under stones be Caier!

she accurately prophesies that Elizabeth will one day
need her tutelage in cursing Richard.

According to Rossiter's analysis of this play's curse-
plotted structure, curses provide dramatic irony in the
form of "verbal *peripeteia*" (p. 5). He divides the play
into five curse movements. The major part of the first
(which includes all of act I) we have just examined. The
second movement (II and III, i–iv) includes King Edward's feeble peacemaking, Buckingham's self-curse, the
lamentation after the king's death, and the fall of Margaret's curse on Rivers, Grey, Vaughan and Hastings.
The third movement (III, v–IV, iii) includes the Glouces-
ter-Buckingham plot for the crown, Anne's meeting of
her own curse as she is called to be queen, Richard's
casting off of Buckingham, and the murder of the princes.
It is the fourth movement (IV, iv–V, i) which especially
interests us: in it Buckingham meets his curse, the three
queens lament together, and Margaret displays her curse-
satire for the last time. (Rossiter's last division includes
only V, ii–iv at Bosworth Field, the fall of the curse on
Richard, and the epilogue to the War of the Roses.)

One of the longest scenes in Shakespeare, IV, iv features Richard's "wooing" of Elizabeth's good favor in
his desire to marry her daughter. Tillyard calls the courting "a prodigious affair" that must be an "afterthought"
because it "leads nowhere."[19] Shakespeare evidently liked

[19] Eustace M. W. Tillyard, *Shakespeare's History Plays* (1946),
p. 214; here Tillyard tries to upset the traditional interpretation,
as given by E. K. Chambers, that Elizabeth tricks Richard in this
scene. As noted by Alice Perry Wood, *The Stage History of Shakespeare's Richard the Third* (1965), p. 85, Cibber's influential eigh-
teenth-century revision of the play made the old interpretation
explicit by adding an aside of Elizabeth's; Cibber also greatly cut
down this scene which was to so fascinate Lamb.

to write wooing scenes, but we must assume that he never
inserted them gratuitously; we must look for the meaning
of this one in its context, which is a thick fabric of variously contending modes of speech, crucial among which
is curse language. Though the wooing leads directly to
nothing in the plot, it has the strategic effect of making
Richard curse himself. To understand why this happens
we must begin with Margaret.

Newly hopeful of Richard's fall because of Henry Tudor's uprising, she infuses the first part of the scene with
her incantational mode. Fluchère characterizes the style
of the scene in these terms:

In this great static scene, until Margaret leaves the stage, we
have as it were an orchestration of grandeur which only a
rhetoric so formal could achieve. It is brought about by the
repetition of motifs, the alternation of reproaches, the similarity of the complaints, the parallelism of the situations and
the depth of the personal feelings, which are first opposed to
each other and then join forces. The grand speech of Queen
Margaret—expert in curses, as Queen Elizabeth calls her—is
the perfection of this proud, haughty, nostalgic and strictly
balanced style.[20]

Before her exit at line 125 Margaret's every word aims
at directing the emotional force of the duchess' and Elizabeth's undifferentiated misery at Richard, for here Margaret incarnates the spirit of vengeance—earthly and
divine.

The force of the triple lamentation depends on the
depiction of the enmity that has hitherto kept these
women apart. Just as England's military rebels unite
under Henry Tudor, so its variously wronged aristocrats

[20] Henri Fluchère, *Shakespeare* (1953), p. 164.

unite under Margaret. Once strong on the battlefield, she now fires her weapons of rhymed, charmlike couplet-asides before she reveals herself to the two sorrowful women:

> *Hover about her. Say that right for right*
> *Hath dimm'd your infant morn to aged night...*
> *Plantagenet doth quit Plantagenet;*
> *Edward for Edward pays a dying debt.*
>   (IV, iv, 15–16, 20–21)

Joining them, she then draws their causes together by using the magic inherent in the incantational repetition of names:

> *I had an Edward, till a Richard killed him;*
> *I had a Harry, till a Richard killed him;*
> *Thou hadst an Edward, till a Richard killed him;*
> *Thou hast a Richard, till a Richard killed him.*
>   (40–43)

In spite of the duchess' objection that Margaret was responsible for the deaths of her husband Richard and son Rutland, Margaret rallies their moral loathing of Richard Crookback through the metaphoric magic that makes him a dog, a "carnal cur"

> *... that had his teeth before his eyes,*
> *To worry lambs and lap their gentle blood.*
>   (49–50)

When she powerfully concludes with

> *Earth gapes, hell burns, fiends roar, saints pray,*
> *To have him suddenly conveyed from hence.*

> *Cancel his bond of life, dear God, I pray,*
> *That I may live to say, 'The dog is dead.'*
>
> (75–78)

Elizabeth suddenly remembers Margaret's prophecy in
I, iii that she would need her help in cursing. Margaret
triumphs at her own accuracy (lines 82–115) and gloats
that now when Elizabeth begs her to "teach me how to
curse mine enemies," she will only leave the following
bitter and ironic advice before going off to France:

> *Forbear to sleep the night, and fast the day;*
> *Compare dead happiness with living woe;*
> *Think that thy babes were sweeter than they were*
> *And he that slew them fouler than he is.*
> *Bett'ring thy loss makes the bad causer worse;*
> *Revolving this will teach thee how to curse.*
>
> (118–123)

She refuses to "quicken" Elizabeth's self-acknowledgedly
"dull words" with her sharp ones. She leaves Elizabeth
only with Richard's mother as ally.

Elizabeth finally sees one value in Margaret's satiric
curse language, the cathartic:

> *Windy attorneys to their client woes,*
> *Airy succeeders of intestate joys,*
> *Poor breathing orators of miseries,*
> *Let them have scope! Though what they will impart*
> *Help nothing else, yet do they ease the heart.*
>
> (126–131)

Elizabeth here refers to that simple, personal catharsis
felt by the curser-satirist which we discussed at the beginning of Chapter I. The old duchess, however, suggests

that under the proper conditions cursing can accomplish
more than the mere release of vengeful emotions:

> *Go with me,*
> *And in the breath of bitter words let's smother*
> *My damned son that thy two sweet sons smother'd.*
> (132–134)

Either magically or metaphorically, cursing can kill and
thereby influence the play's plot and the ultimate aesthetic effect. When these two then pounce on Richard,
using Margaret's mode, shouting accusations and the
dread names of all those he has killed, he has alarums
sounded to drown them out, so as not to let "the heavens
hear these telltale women / Rail on the Lord's anointed."
The duchess has to promise to speak gently before he
will hear her but manages to exit with this powerful, well-
formed curse.[21]

> *Either thou wilt die by God's just ordinance*
> *Ere from this war thou turn a conqueror,*
> *Or I with grief and extreme age shall perish*
> *And never more behold thy face again.*
> *Therefore take with thee my most grievous curse,*
> *Which in the day of battle tire thee more*
> *Than all the complete armour that thou wearest!*
> *My prayers on the adverse party fight,*
> *And there the little souls of Edward's children*
> *Whisper the spirits of thine enemies*

---

[21] Rice, p. 147, finds that the *either-or* curse structure has Senecan origins, and Rehyer, p. 240, says that this mother's curse,
"reniant son fils est assez atroce pour impressioner Richard, au
fond très superstitieux, déchaîner les remords qu'ils a réuissi
jusqu'alors à refouler, et l'affaibler."

And promise them success and victory!
Bloody thou art, bloody will be thy end;
Shame serves thy life and doth thy death attend.

(184–196)

Elizabeth, now left alone to deal with Richard's out-
rageous "courting" (the audience sensing that she will
not do as badly as Anne did earlier) is in full sympathy
with the duchess, but knows she lacks the professional
curser's gift: "Though far more cause, yet much less
spirit to curse / Abides in me," she says, and proceeds to
tackle the fiend for 230 lines with her plain power of
logic. It should not be surprising that a character named
Queen Elizabeth receives Shakespeare's unqualified approval; in this scene Elizabeth triumphs when she appears
to lose; she has the wit and diplomacy of her more famous
namesake, and her careful nature avoids the dangerous
curse mode with which she has just shown great sympathy. She has learned her lesson from Margaret, as Lorentz
Eckhoff observes,[22] but, as I read the scene, instead of
making use of her lesson by cursing Richard outright,
she does so by trapping him into cursing himself.

She mockingly points out (lines 200–290) the absurdity
and impossibility of his request that she put in a good
word for him with her daughter (another Elizabeth, mentioned at the end of IV, iii, as being sought also by Richmond, so that whoever gets her gets England). When he
argues that he will make her queen again through the
person of her daughter, she responds, in a brilliant exchange of stychomithia, that no style of language can be
compatible with such evil content (lines 357–360). He

[22] Lorentz Eckhoff, *Shakespeare: Spokesman of the Third Estate*
(1954), p. 101.

objects, "your reasons are too shallow and too quick," but she punningly points out that they are really "deep and dead (poor infants)," and forces him to seek an oath by which to swear his sincerity. His "by my George, my garter, and my crown—" she proves "Profaned, dishonoured, . . . usurped"; with cold logic she disallows his swearing by "The world," his "father's death," himself, God, or "the time to come." Richard's only recourse is to swear by himself, and he dares the resulting self-curse[23] to its last incantational couplet:

> *Myself myself confound!*
> *Heaven and fortune bar me happy hours!*
> *Day, yield me not thy light, nor, night, thy rest!*
> *Be opposite all planets of good luck*
> *To my proceeding if, with dear heart's love,*
> *Immaculate devotion, holy thoughts,*
> *I tender not thy beauteous princely daughter!*
> *In her consists my happiness and thine;*
> *Without her, follows to myself and thee,*
> *Herself, the land, and many a Christian soul,*
> *Death, desolation, ruin, and decay.*
> *It cannot be avoided but by this;*
> *It will not be avoided but by this.*

(399–410)

[23] A. E. Crawley, "Cursing and Blessing," *Encyclopaedia of Religion and Ethics* (1961), p. 373, explains that the oath is essentially a conditional self-curse; moreover, "the magic power inherent in the cursing words is its essence" (Crawley, "The Oath: Introductory and Primitive," ibid., p. 430). The Hebrew words for curse and oath are almost interchangeable; Hebrew code regards the false oath as one of the seven capital sins (Maurice A. Canney, "The Oath: Semitic," ibid., pp. 437–438.) Christ made strong injunctions against misused oaths and the medieval church carefully controlled them (W. E. Beet, "The Oath: New Testament and Christian," ibid., p. 434–435.)

Elizabeth has won. Though she pretends to succumb to this tempting devil, who triumphs at her exit, "Relenting fool, and shallow, changing woman!" she has only promised to write and let him know her daughter's decision. From this point on Richard is a doomed man—self-doomed. Indeed, even the rest of this scene is devoted to the bad news of Richmond's gathering forces in the north.

Richard has cursed himself with sleeplessness in strange accord with Margaret's I, iii, curse: "No sleep close up that deadly eye of thine." She has plotted what he had to trigger. His bad dreams at Bosworth Field (V, iii) only dramatize through ghosts the realization of Margaret's earlier curse: "The worm of conscience still begnaw thy soul!" The ghosts of all those he has murdered curse him in succession, "Despair and die," in what M. C. Randolph calls "an interesting example of coterie curse in the Celtic manner."[24] His infamous conscience grows "a thousand several tongues" and, his own greatest judge, he condemns himself to the death Richmond will execute the next day. Thus Margaret's curse goes through the medium of the Duchess of York, is manipulated by Elizabeth, and is set off by Richard before it finally works.

III

The arch-curser, Margaret, represents the satirist at a primitive stage. In tracing the effectiveness of her curses we actually are studying the essence of satire used in

---

[24] Her dissertation, cited by Rice, p. 209, who explains that the rationale and ghosts are Senecan or Christian in origin and only the coterie aspect Celtic, as in group prayers, excommunication and chanted curses.

drama. Thus *Richard III* completes a satiric catharsis because it fulfills Margaret's curse—the verbalization of her
hatred and censure of Richard.

H. B. Charleton observes that this play leaves the audience assured of the arrest of evil-doers, serene, com-
forted.[25] As for the evil-doers, the play sets up clear
ethical camps: there is no doubt of Richard's evil, or that
he is a tyrant who must, according even to Elizabethan
rules, be overthrown; obversely, there is no doubt that
Margaret and Elizabeth and the duchess, with all the
wronged Lancasters and Yorks they represent, are now
in the right, whatever they may have been in the past.
Thus we in the audience are made to temporarily share
the moral values of *Richard III*. We are outraged by
Richard's every Machiavellian act and (notwithstanding
our perverse admiration of him) must be anxious that
forces oppose him. We then experience a vicarious release[26] of hatred and censure with the cursers as they
speak; our hearts are "eased"—as even the noncontent-
ious Elizabeth observed about railing against evil. The
very presence of the cursers in the play opens our satiric
valve. Their great effectiveness in the plot taps off all our
railing, reforming steam. Curses touching off self-curses
touching off death cure the mimetic world before us. The
bloodiest play in Shakespeare is not likely to incite regi-

[25] Henry Buckley Charlton, *Shakespearean Tragedy* (1961),
p. 39.
[26] Elliott, *Power of Satire*, p. 140, conjectures that the railer
(Thersites archetype) "is privileged to abuse whom he will because
he affords author and audience vicarious satisfaction as he attacks
figures of authority. Momentarily, perhaps unconsciously, we identify with him and so gain release of frustrated aggressive feelings
with which we are charged."

cide or murder outside of the theater.[27] Release replaces
frustration and we come away from the theater cured—
"good" peaceful citizens instead of provocative satirists
or agitators.

Bloody battle is the most primitive type of manifesta-
tion of satiric catharsis on stage, quite fitting for the
primitive state of the play's satire. There are, however,
adumbrations here of the satirist-satirized theme, which
is apparently essential to the liberation of satire from
its magical, and therefore nonrational and nonliterary,
stage.[28] Renaissance society, of course, is beginning to
doubt the very basis of Margaret's powers—magic. The
efficacy of her curses would seem to reinforce the traditional fear of the magical-religious forces, but, after all,
a man, and not a curse, actually kills Richard, and psychology replaces magic when "conscience" mediates
between curse and death. The primitive satirist exists
in great insecurity in a no longer primitive society because
of the questions surrounding his social position.

Margaret also flirts with rejection on purely dramatic
grounds: though she has our moral sympathy, she does

[27] Alice P. Wood, *The Stage History of Shakespeare's King Richard the Third* (1965), p. 170, notes the play was "the favorite of
strolling comedians, inaugurated the Shakespearean drama in
America in primitive colonial structures, was played for Cherokee
Indians, before the Hawaiian king, in German-American theatres,
under the guise of 'moral lectures,' as travesty, burlesque, circus at-
traction, by children's and women's companies. It has been depended upon for benefits, has always been a favorite as a first
performance."

[28] Elliott, *Power of Satire*, p. 98, interpreting from E. Kris and
E. H. Gombrich, "The Principles of Caricature" in *Psychoanalytic
Explorations in Art* (1952), pp. 189–203. See Elliott, pp. 130–222, for
the satirist-satirized theme in misanthrope literature.

not always have our dramatic sympathy. She tempts comical stage rejection of the berated-fool variety, for instance, when she enters like a hag (I, iii) and demands subservience from the royalty about her. We even have cause to doubt her overall morality when the recollection at I, iii, 194 of York's curse on her (from *3 Henry VI*) brings with it the memory of her ugly character throughout the first three parts of the cycle. Her objectionable nature indeed continues to show throughout the play as she reveals her relentless bitterness against Elizabeth, who is sympathetically presented, and as she leaves for France in a continued frenzy of hatred.

Shakespeare finishes his noninflammatory political drama, then, by gently undercutting his triumphant satirist, thereby rejecting as political credo the mode of insurrection she champions even while condoning her specific acts. Thus the satirist-curser's unpleasant character and her angry, ignominious (though victorious) exit *begin* to suggest the punishment and casting out of the mock king or railer in the Roman Saturnalia.[29] But in this play it is still plot effectiveness, and not this ritualized rejection, that brings about the satiric catharsis. The satirist-satirized theme will function far more importantly in the case of Falstaff, which I will examine next.

Before leaving the clearer air of the curse in drama for the cloudy sea of satire in drama, it may be well to draw out the metaphoric implications of the anthropological fact of cursing. Traditionally, a holy name or blessing often followed the curse to neutralize it. Inasmuch as

[29] James George Frazer, *The Scapegoat* [*Golden Bough*, vol. 9] (1955), pp. 345 ff; Elliott, p. 80, discusses Frazer in the context of satiric theory.

the play replaces the ritual, we can expect that either the curse in it will "work" or it will be exorcised. The stage curser such as Margaret curses the evil stage character, but an uncomfortable magic of aesthetics functions to make her curse include all ambitious, unscrupulous people *in the audience* who would cause political turmoil for selfish reasons.

In the preface to *The Battle of the Books* Swift writes:

Satire is a sort of glass, wherein beholders do generally discover everybody's face but their own; which is the chief reason for that kind of reception it meets in the world, and that so very few are offended with it.

In *Richard III* Shakespeare makes it easy for us to see Richard in the glass instead of ourselves. Because the moral delineations are so clear, we only side with the satirist instead of also seeing ourselves as the reprehensible; we thereby preclude the necessity of curse exorcism. The dramatist, in other words, builds in the exorcism by fictionalizing the mimetic world, i.e., rendering its moral situation unambiguously and thereby distancing it from reality.

"But if it should happen otherwise," Swift goes on, if we *should* recognize ourselves in the satiric glass,

the danger is not great . . . for anger and fury, though they add strength to the sinews of the body, yet are found to relax those of the mind, and to render all its efforts feeble and impotent.

This is precisely what happens in most satire that receives our aesthetic approval. Even if we feel the lash of the curse, we immediately find a way—the author provides it—of exorcising that curse: we laugh, we jeer, we trot out the scapegoat, we say it is a fiction.

3: The Rejection of
Falstaffian Satire

By the time he wrote *Henry IV* Shakespeare had already gone through what Sigurd Burckhardt describes[1] as the modernizing experience of writing *King John*. The satire therefore becomes more recognizable as such because the author has developed it, as well as his ideas on the world order, out of a more "primitive" stage. In the early histories a supernaturally gifted speaker cursed against a relatively clear moral disorder; in the later histories a satirist's wit challenges an already crumbling world order. And it is probably in the nature of this transition from magic to art that actual belief in the destructive power of abusive language must wither in order that satiric wit may flourish.[2]

We all recognize Falstaff as a wit whose language embodies some kind of threat to constituted authority; the prince's rejection of him can be important only in this context. Our task here is to uncover the nature of the Falstaffian satiric attack in the *Henry IV* plays in order to show how and to what extent the disruption it arouses is purged through the dramatic structure.

[1] Sigurd Burckhardt, *Shakespearean Meanings* (1968), p. 117.
[2] Robert C. Elliott, *The Power of Satire* (1960), p. 98.

I say "Falstaff*ian*" because Sir Jack alone does not quite satisfy as the satirist of these plays. From tradition we expect the satirist to be an angry, hating man. This Falstaff is not.[3] We also expect to hear the voice of an outraged moralist. While there is much strong, conventional moralizing in *Henry IV* it certainly does not come from Falstaff—though he has much to say *against* traditional concepts of virtue and honor. Outside of Falstaff's wit, the only trait traditional in the satirist is his tendency toward gross or seemingly immoral acts and words.

On this point let us step away from the plays for a moment to investigate the distasteful and conflicting qualities of our generalized satirist, of our immoral moralist. The Renaissance belief that the satirist originated from the Greek satyr helps to explain how our character became so self-contradictory.

In the interludes at the Greek *tragoidia* presentations the satyrs were privileged to abuse and scoff since they appeared incognito—costumed actors freely played the roles of the mythic satyrs. They could rail and criticize publicly with little regard for established morality or for repercussions when divested of the satyr disguise. George Wither makes one such Renaissance "satyrist" describe himself quite frankly:

> I'me sent abroad the World, to purge
> Mans vile Abuses with my scourge;

[3] Oscar James Campbell, *Shakespeare's Satire* (1963), p. x, says, "Falstaff's descriptions lack the ill nature and moral zeal informing the works which served as their models," yet they are variations "of a well-established satiric convention" which "throw a flood of light upon Shakespeare's critical temper."

> *Oft I make my Master sport,*
> *When men sinne to lash them for't.*
>   *An Executioner am I,*
>   *Of Lust, and wanton Venery.*
> *Thus are vices scourged by mee,*
> *Yet my selfe from vice not free;*
>   *Like to Sumners that cite others,*
>   *When themselves defile their mothers.*[4]

The vileness of the last simile is not an unusual association for the hybrid satyrist of the period.

The first Boarshead Tavern scene of *1 Henry IV* features a man—not Falstaff—who boasts a virtuoso hybrid
character. It begins with the curious business of Prince
Hal's taunting of Francis, whose inability to communicate
through language is exposed. Hal has his accomplice Poins
repeatedly call "Francis" from another room while the
prince tosses double-talk questions at the poor apprentice
tapster who consequently becomes so confused that he
can only repeat "Anon, Anon." When Hal and Poins finally both call his name at once poor Francis cannot move
until his boss, the Vintner, finally scolds him away. Poins
then asks what was "the issue" of the jest; Hall replies, "I
am now of all humours that have showed themselves since
the old days of goodman Adam to the pupil age of this
present twelve o'clock at midnight" (II, iv, 104–107).

What new humor has he just added to his repertoire?
The sequel clarifies. When the victim reenters, Hal asks,
"What's o'clock Francis?" The distraught boy cries out,

---

[4] Quoted by Eugene Waith, *The Pattern of Tragicomedy in
Beaumont and Fletcher* (1952), p. 58, in a section to which my
paragraph on the satyrs is indebted.

"Anon, anon, sir" and flees. By using the satirist's magical device of incantationally repeating the victim's name, Hal has "destroyed" Francis. It is thus the satirist's humor that he has exercised so much to his satisfaction.

As if to emphasize this, Hal in conclusion mocks Francis's lack of eloquence and likens the boy to a parrot. Having reduced the miserable creature to the level of an animal, the prince appears to us somewhat cruel and disagreeable—though admittedly witty. That he is acting the satirist in this scene is further clarified when he adds to his anti-Francis tirade, without a pause, the following seeming non sequitur:

> I am not yet of Percy's mind, the Hotspur of the North; he that kills me some six or seven dozen of Scots at a breakfast, washes his hands, and says to his wife, 'Fie upon this quiet life! I want work.' 'O my sweet Harry,' says she, 'how many hast thou kill'd today?' 'Give my roan horse a drench,' says he, and answers 'Some fourteen,' an hour after, 'a trifle, a trifle.'
>
> (114–120)

The tone of the passage is satiric, its literary model the Theophrastan character. The mocking hyperbole of Hal's attack undercuts Hotspur's fierceness, drains it of reality. But a crucial difference of course exists between satiric attack and physical attack: one kills metaphorically while the other kills in earnest. If the prince's satiric murder of Francis has appeared cruel, then we are forced right here to compare it with the greater cruelty and ultimate unplayfulness of the military murdering which will shape the prince's future career.

Hal, like the Renaissance "satyrist," is something of a hybrid character himself, a typically immoral moralist, albeit in a princely costume new to the tradition. As prince, soldier and upholder of established justice, Hal conveys all of the sternly moralistic ideas we expect from a "satyrist." As tavern brawler, thief and wearer of disguises he fulfills some of the more unseemly expectations of the role. In fact, Hal's every association with Falstaff's world serves to further the undermining of that moral structure of the Establishment to which he in his other life is pledged. His Falstaffian life provides a paradigm for rebellion,[5] the true subject of the plays.

The first scene depicts King Henry explaining the troubles plaguing his "unquiet reign." The next, in Hal's quarters, exists precisely to show us that the royal-Falstaffian relationship epitomizes that internal rebellion which in Shakespeare's view must have been so much more deeply disruptive than the explicit rebellion of Hotspur. Scene ii is actually framed by references to (scene i) and depiction of (scene iii) Hotspur's political rebellion. It, then, must depict the king's greatest worry: that filial and societal rebellion which curses his reign. We know this, not only from the scene's content, but also from the preparation for it at the end of *Richard II*. At the very moment of his victory over Richard, Henry had named his own curse:

> *Can no man tell me of my unthrifty son?*
> *'Tis full three months since I did see him last.*
> *If any plague hang over us, 'tis he.*

[5] Lily Bess Campbell, *Shakespeare's Histories* (1958), p. 218, sees Henry IV as the proper subject for a play built around the theme of rebellion.

I would to God, my lords, he might be found.
Inquire at London 'mongst the taverns there,
For there, they say, he daily doth frequent,
With unrestrained loose companions,
Even such, they say, as stand in narrow lanes
And beat our watch and rob our passengers,
Which he, young wanton and effeminate boy,
Takes on the point of honour to support
So dissolute a crew.

(V, iii, 1–12)

In the tavern world of Misrule[6] Hal will enact with Falstaff the part of God's scourge. Shakespeare manipulated
his chronicle material so as to *interpret* Hal's historically
dissolute activities as the punishing vengeance for his
father's guilt.[7] Much of the abusive language issuing from
the Falstaffian union can be seen as a satire against the
king and all he represents.

Falstaff and Hal are united in the early parts of the
play in a relationship akin to what biologists call "mu-
tualistic symbiosis": these two very dissimilar organisms
live together in a partnership wherein both "host" and
"guest" benefit. Because their cooperation in this tavern
life is so complete, I treat them as one being, the Satirist.
Symbiosis permits them together to satirize the status
quo in a way which would have been impossible for
either one separately. They give and take between them
the satirist's attributes—his Roman linguistic talents as
well as his reputedly Greek moral inconsistencies.

[6] Cesar Lombardi Barber, *Shakespeare's Festive Comedy* (1959),
ch. 8.

[7] L. B. Campbell, *Histories*, p. 222, notes that Bolingbroke is a
character needing to be purged.

Act II (Part 1), almost wholly devoted to the depiction of this Satirist in action, shows us what each half contributes to the whole entity. Falstaff, first of all, has the natural magic, i.e., the mysterious literary gift of wit. In II, ii, at Gadshill, when Hal refuses to get him a horse, Falstaff first utters a wittily destructive wish, "Go hang thyself in thine own heir-apparent garters!" and then threatens to lampoon the tricksters, clinching the threat with a self-curse: "An I have not ballads made on you all, and sung to filthy tunes, let a cup of sack be my poison."[8] He is inclined to satire, though he, evidently, would not make the really destructive verses himself.

In *Shakespeare's Satire*, O. J. Campbell calls Falstaff the "genial hilarious satiric commentator" of the *Henry IV* plays (p. 23). He sees Falstaff's impersonation of the king in II, iv as "a direct ridicule of euphuism, still regarded by some great ones of Shakespeare's day as the prose proper to courtly speech" (p. 18). He finds Falstaff a devastating exposer of the hollowness of the glories of battle in IV, ii, and a trenchant critic of chivalric ideals of war for the Elizabethan gentleman in V, i. Falstaff's soliloquy on Justice Shallow (Part 2, III, ii, 325–343) is a satiric "caricature which at once bites and tickles" (p. 21). Yet Campbell notes that Falstaff is somehow deficient in the fervidly reformatory aim typical of the satirist (p. 19). Enid Welsford, in discussing comedy as the expression of the spirit of the Fool, divides Aristotelian comedy (depicting men worse than they are) into

[8] James G. Rice, "Shakespeare's Curse" (1947), p. 175, notes that eight of the twenty-five instances of the "plague curse" in Shakespeare are Falstaff's, "making it very clear that this speech tag is part of his characterization."

two kinds: the comic view delights in the vagaries of un-
heroic characters and even admires them for their suc-
cessful evasion of the moral issue, while the moralistic
view points out that they ought to be different and pro-
duces satire.[9] For this moralistic component in our com-
posite Satirist we turn to the young prince.

From beginning to end Hal's speech is thoroughly
pervaded with conventionally moralistic language. Even
before his explicitly moral "I know you all . . ." monologue (I, ii) he makes clear his theoretical position. The
first railing speech of the play is his, trenchantly directed
against his companion:

> Thou art so fat-witted with drinking of old sack,
> and unbuttoning thee after supper, and sleeping
> upon benches after noon, that thou has forgotten
> to demand that truly which thou wouldest know.
> What a devil hast thou to do with the time of day?
> Unless hours were cups of sack, and minutes capons,
> and clocks the tongues of bawds, and dials the signs
> of leaping houses, and the blessed sun himself a
> fair hot wench in flame-coloured taffeta, I see no
> reason why thou shouldst be so superfluous to de-
> mand the time of the day.
>
> (I, ii, 2–13)

In response to Falstaff's oblique pleas for social reform,
Hal wittily threatens him with references to the constable
(I, ii, 42)—representative of established justice; this al-
lusion foreshadows Hal's espousing of the Lord Chief
Justice as counselor-father figure in place of Falstaff in

[9] Enid Welsford, *The Fool: His Social and Literary History*
(1961), p. 321.

Part 2, V, ii. In a little wit combat of insulting similes, even Falstaff has to congratulate Hal on his satiric skills: "Thou hast the most unsavory similes, and art indeed the most comparative, rascalist, sweet young prince" (I, ii, 89). Even though Hal himself suggests the Gadshill thievery escapade, it is only Poins's plot to rob the robbers that persuades him to participate in the thievery. It is noteworthy that as soon as Falstaff exits, Hal drops the railing, satiric mode and lapses into a more straightforward style that culminates in the lofty monologue on his reformation. I interpret this shift as showing that Hal as satirist depends on the presence and cooperation of Falstaff in a relationship overtly pitted against traditional values, but destined, through its disintegration, to eventuate in their support.

After the Gadshill episode, Hal's moralistic bite sharpens. When Falstaff exaggerates the number of his attackers, Hal rails at him:

> These lies are like their father that begets them—gross as a mountain, open, palpable. Why, thou claybrain'd guts, thou knotty-pated fool, thou whoreson obscene greasy tallow-catch—
>
> (II, iv, 249–253)

So violent is the attack that Falstaff has to stop Hal by reminding him, "Ah, no more of that, Hal, an thou lovest me!" (312). Satire expresses hatred. Falstaff foresees the prince's potential power to destroy with a word their tensely maintained symbiosis. He must ward off the moralistic hatred and censure; he must remind the prince of love and deflect the increasingly fierce royal criticism. This he does successfully when he redirects Hal's con-

tinued railing about his obesity (II, iv. 357 ff) toward
their mutual enemies, Percy and Glendower, of whom
threatening news has just arrived. They proceed to a kind
of wit combat at Owen Glendower's expense. And by the
time III, i opens with Glendower, Percy and their wives
on stage, this faction has already been undermined by
the play's satiric team. The political rebels, one might
say, eventually die because their characters have been attacked in the Boarshead Tavern by a powerful Satirist.

But we know it is the sword and not the word that literally kills. And Hal must swear to bathe himself in literal
blood for the "good" of king and country. To do so, from
his view and his father's, he must "banish" the tavern-
world of satire because Hal as satirist has been of the
absolutist type characterized by highly moralistic ideals.
In one famous speech Falstaff shows that to banish
Peto, Bardolph and "plump Jack" is to "banish all the
world." Absolutist Hal grimly replies, "I do, I will." The
dissolution of our symbiotic Satirist looms closer.[10]

If Hal represents the moral absolutist in satire, Falstaff
represents something disarmingly different—the skeptic
satirist. The former upholds traditional values while the
latter unceasingly debunks, destroys and undermines
them. What has Falstaff stood for in the first two acts?
In his first appearance he suggests some "reforms" he
looks forward to during Hal's kingship: the abolition of

---

[10] Discussing duality in the many father-son combinations in
these plays, Ernst Kris, *Psychoanalytic Explorations in Art* (1952),
p. 278, says, "Impulses pertaining to one situation have thus been
divided between two personages; but though in the triangles the
characters are paired and contrasted, each of the play's personages
transcends the bondage to his function in this thematic configura-
tion. They have all outgrown the symmetry which they serve, into
the fullness of life."

"Grace"—presumably both social and religious (I, ii, 20);
the recognition of individual law—for men like himself
(lines 23 ff); and the abolition of capital punishment
(line 55). These all presuppose most alarming *anti-values*
which attack established religious, social and legal systems from the philosophic position of the Renaissance
skeptic.

Richard H. Popkin notes that Rabelais in Book III,
chapter 36 of *Gargantua et Pantagruel* and Molière in *Le
Marriage Forcé*, satirically dramatize the renaissance of
interest in the ancient skeptical philosophy of Pyrrho
caused by the rediscovery of the writings of Sextus Em-
piricus (200 A.D.).[11] According to Popkin, this revival in
skepticism from 1500–1650 played a strategic part in the
Reformation because of its anti-Aristotelian bias and
distrust in reason as opposed to faith. Culminating in
Montaigne's *Apologie de Raimond Sebond*, Renaissance
skepticism stressed suspension of judgment on all propo-
sitions; "in this state of complete doubt," Montaigne
says, "the Pyrrhonists live according to nature and custom"—an attitude he considers compatible with religion
(Popkin, p. 43). But ethical relativism and "the bottom-
less pit of complete doubt" (p. 53) characterize the position. From Montaigne on, the skeptical challenge was to
spur the Counter-Reformation and culminate in the philosophy of Descartes.

S. L. Bethell makes a case for Falstaff as a hypocritical
Puritan—to the Elizabethans representing disorder for
church and state.[12] One of Falstaff's models was the no-

[11] Richard H. Popkin, *The History of Skepticism From Erasmus
to Descartes* (1964), pp. 21–22.
[12] Samuel L. Bethell, "The Comic Element in Shakespeare's
Histories" (1952), pp. 92–99.

torious Lollard Sir John Oldcastle. Falstaff is preoccupied
with the subject of repentance, loses his voice singing
loud anthems, and his companion Mistress Quickly attends on the Puritan divine, "Master Dumble." Bethell
goes on to suggest that as a Vice character Falstaff attempts to overthrow moral and metaphysical order
through his language of witty inversion. He stresses the
evacuation from life of all conventional spiritual significance and emphasizes the spiritual value of secular vo-
cations (which was a major part of Reformation theology)
and the extreme Protestant repudiation of meritorious
works. Because Bethell sides with Dover Wilson and Tillyard in the "anti-sentimental" view of Falstaff, he condemns Falstaff for his Puritan leanings and considers him
as a villainous Vice character. I would suggest that Falstaff cannot be brushed aside because he is discovered
to use false arguments and the "materialistic inversion
by rhetorical fallacy." His dramatic value remains. In
fact, the idea of Falstaff as Puritan fits well into the larger
view of Falstaff as Renaissance skeptic and is by no means
clearly repudiated by Shakespeare.

While this interpretation is not vital to our discussion
of satire in the plays, it does help to suggest the direction
of Shakespeare's "disruptive" impulses, as dramatized
through his Falstaffian satire. Writing in Elizabethan England about pre-Reformation political turmoils, Shakespeare could well be "on the side" of the Falstaffian
Protest and mean quite clearly to throw doubt on the
certainty Henry V claims in such piously old-fashioned
terms as he takes over his father's unsteady throne.
Shakespeare as satirist is thus far removed from the
traditionalist most critics see behind these history plays.

Bethell (p. 100) even points to their "principle of multi-consciousness" which forces the audience to recognize very contemporary problems mixed with the dramatization of chronicle history. Everyone in Shakespeare's audience would have known what chaos was to follow the so-called ideal hero-king, Henry V, with his vaunted stabilizing effect on the country. Still, Shakespeare could not take an unequivocal stand with his rebels because along with the growing religious and political uncertainty that Falstaff championed came dread political upheaval. But this, after all, was precisely the problem of the Renaissance.

The growing disruption of the delicately balanced satiric symbiosis appears in III, iii at the Boarshead Tavern as the conflict between the two differing modes of satire, the absolutist's and the skeptic's. Just before this scene Hal has had to swear to his father that he will bathe himself in the blood of war to prove his princely allegiance to king and kingdom. He then enters the tavern with stern military matters in mind, armed with the moralistic language of raillery to use against Falstaff's antimoralistic satire. Falstaff's vow to repent at the beginning of the scene irreverently parodies the prince's repentance before the king which we have just witnessed. Before Hal enters, Falstaff has taunted Bardolph for amusement and later, to discredit her testimony against him, he insults the Hostess by likening her to "stewed" prunes. Hal, on a recruiting mission, becomes engaged in spite of his intentions by Falstaff's nihilistic wit but finally combats him with this moralistic, abusive rally:

there's no room for faith, truth, nor honesty in this
bosom of thine. It is all fill'd up with guts and mid-
riff. Charge an honest woman with picking thy
pocket? Why, thou whoreson, impudent, emboss'd
rascal, if there were anything in thy pocket but tavern reckonings, memorandums of bawdy houses,
and one poor pennyworth of sugar candy to make
thee long-winded—if thy pockets were enrich'd
with any other injuries but these, I am a villain. And
yet you will stand to it; you will not pocket up
wrong. Art thou not ashamed?

(171–184)

The skeptical destruction of rational values, however,
wins this round when Falstaff then reminds us that human virtue fell with Adam and makes Hal admit he himself had picked the pocket. After this victory for antivalues the team is reunited, only to go off to war—which
Hal here lets his friends believe may be another field for
their shared unscrupulous pranks. Hal has no rebuke for
Falstaff's suggestion that he exercise his new favor with
the king by immediately robbing the exchequer.

Throughout the rest of Part 1 the symbiosis not only
resists the pressures of war, but Falstaff's disruptive values actually make their mark on the warring Establishment. We get a chance to see some of the play's satiric
barbs hit home as Falstaff makes a merry mockery of
battle. Thus the destructive emotions earlier aroused by
the attacks of the Satirist (Falstaff-Hal) are mimetically
purged in this section. We vicariously enact with Falstaff
the disruption of the war machine, and the play leaves us
in equilibrium, our inflamed hatred and censure having

been cathected (to borrow a term from Freud) by stage representations of reality.

In IV, ii Falstaff happily admits that he has damnably misused the king's power of impressment by hiring only the most ragged beggars instead of strong young men. His grim, twice repeated tag for the crew, "Food for powder," bitingly explains the antiheroic direction of his disloyal actions that so accord with his previously expressed antivalues. (In a similar conscription scene of Part 2 [III, ii][13] Falstaff makes the act of "pricking" his recruits accompany his verbal satire. These actions correspond to the ritualistic movements accompanying the primitive satirist's curse; as the magical gesture strengthened the curse, so the recruitment of beggars supports the satire.) The absurd contrast between the appearance of Falstaff's men and the glorious way Vernon has described Hal's troops to enemy Hotspur (in IV, i) undermines the officially proposed heroic value of war. Moreover, by prolonging the recruitment scene, Shakespeare further explores the existing evils of that miserable poverty which drives poor men to sell themselves to the war machine.

This social criticism develops in the next scene into the more revolutionary argument against Henry IV as God's rightfully anointed king. The ideology of the political rebels against the king thus parallels and supports the Falstaffian satiric rebellion from within. And the culminating part of the play, the battle at Shrewsbury, then

[13] Samuel L. Bethell, *Shakespeare and the Popular Dramatic Tradition* (1948), p. 50, likens Shakespeare in this scene to Swift: the Falstaffian reference to Elizabethan recruiting methods distances and objectifies them; Gulliver's diminishing and increasing stature reveals human failings more clearly.

shows the rebel Falstaffian antivalues holding their own even as the political rebels fall.

At the start of this last act Hal voices the traditional heroic creed that his father represents: "I have a truant been to chivalry," he cries, and vows to seek single combat against Percy in order to prove his valor and prevent mass bloodshed. But the scene does not end on this high-toned note. Instead, Falstaff openly tells the prince of his qualms before battle. Hal rebukes him with conventionally religious words, "Why, thou owest God a death," and leaves. In soliloquy, Falstaff then ends the scene with his famous "catechism" against honor:

> 'Tis not due yet. I would be loath to pay him before his day. What need I be so forward with him that calls not on me? Well, 'tis no matter; honour pricks me on. Yea, but how if honour prick me off when I come on? How then? Can honour set to a leg? No. Or an arm? No. Or take away the grief of a wound? No. What is honour? A word. What is that word honour? Air. A trim reckoning! Who hath it? He that died a Wednesday. Doth he feel it? No. Doth he hear it? No. 'Tis insensible then? Yea, to the dead. But will it not live with the living? No. Why? Detraction will not suffer it. Therefore I'll none of it. Honour is a mere scutcheon—and so ends my catechism.

> (*1 Henry IV*, V, i, 128–144)

The verbal wit, the parody of affirmative religious catechisms plus the derisive repetition of "honour," carry the satiric thrust of this speech. Its values are those of the skeptic: none are credited but the most immediately perceivable human values such as setting a leg, curing a wound; only sense experience transmits to us a knowable picture of reality; and all rationally conceived concepts—such as honor—are nullified. Thus, as Hal begins to switch out of his role as symbiotic satirist, Falstaff begins to direct antimoralistic verbal attacks at his newly affected heroic mode, just as Hal has hitherto directed moralistic attacks at Falstaff without actually destroying their symbiosis. The brave combat with Hotspur is hereby undercut before it starts.

The pattern continues. Scene ii is heroic, scene iii antiheroic, with Falstaff remarking on the body of Blunt, who died because he dressed as the king, "There's honour for you!"—as if to support his catechism with the evidence of a meaninglessly grinning corpse. With so few words Falstaff attacks the reality of the concept of honor and self-sacrifice in the name of a sanctified spiritual and political leader: the men who dressed as King Henry in order to fool the enemy are now all equal in death to a real dead king. In effect, all men are kings, all mere corpses. Satiric jest again interjects in the heroic war scene where Falstaff offers Hal a bottle of sack as the "pistol" with which to defend himself against Percy. Leaving, Hal throws the bottle at him and their relationship is strained, but Falstaff puns on the enemy's name to reassert his skeptic satirist's position:

> Well, if Percy be alive, I'll pierce him. If he do come in my way, so; if he do not, if I come in his willingly, let him make a carbonado of me. I like not such grinning honour as Sir Walter hath. Give me life; which if I can save, so; if not, honour comes unlook'd for, and there's an end.
>
> (V, iii, 58–64)

When Hotspur dies in his chivalric fight with Hal in scene iv, he regrets the loss of his "proud titles" more than the life itself. Falstaff's speech equating honor to death undercuts the heroism of this declaration. And Hotspur's last words, "No, Percy, thou are dust, And food for—" must remind us of Falstaff's "Food for powder," even as Hal completes the dying sentence, "For worms, brave Percy." Shakespeare interweaves the heroic and the antiheroic, but the emphasis, by virtue of the greater stage value of Falstaff over that of Percy, falls with the antiheroic, the satiric. Brave Percy dead, Shakespeare says, is equal to the most ragged of Falstaff's recruits.

Simultaneously with this "heroic" death, Falstaff's "cowardly" feigned death takes place *on stage* to further rob the former of its heroic value through parodic mime. When Douglas attacks him Falstaff pretends to be dead simply in order to preserve his life. As he says after all exit, "The better part of valour is discretion; in the which better part I have saved my life." Falstaff's "resurrection" based on his ingrained antivalues thus strongly rivals for our sympathy the traditionally pious sentiments Hal voices over the two bodies. And when Hal then discovers a live Jack with a newly wounded dead Hotspur, he reasserts his ties to the whole Falstaffian world by doing grace to this anti-Christ's lies. Because Falstaff alive still means more to Hal than the glory of having killed Hotspur, he lets Falstaff take the prize. Shakespeare makes Hal, and all of us, along with Falstaff, believe in the value of any life over the worth of the dead hero. And it has been the skeptical satirist who has all along argued this position and worked his verbal magic to make it the officially accepted one.

At the end of Part 1, then, the censorious emotions

aroused by satire are purged because of the effective playing out of satiric aggressions. With Falstaff at Hal's side in war, still working his linguistic and ritualistic magic, reform begins to parade itself onstage. Satire begins to "work" as the satirist sees his curses permeate the Establishment.

Henry IV, Part 2 is a very different sort of drama. In his film based on these plays, Orson Welles "directed everything, played everything, in the perspective of the last scene."[14] To argue my case that the Falstaffian threat is a satiric one dependent on the acknowledged power of this type of charmed language, let us begin with the very end of the final scene.

After Hal has repudiated Falstaff with his "I know thee not, old man" speech, his brother, Prince John of Lancaster, reverses the new king's benevolent allowances for his old friends when he says in private to the Lord Chief Justice:

> *I like this fair proceeding of the King's*
> *He hath intent his wonted followers*
> *Shall all be very well provided for;*
> *But all are banish'd till their conversations*
> *Appear more wise and modest to the world.*
>
> > (2 *Henry IV*, V, v, 103–107)

Most reprehensible in the tavern-goers' behavior is their "conversations"—which may be interpreted as that particular mode of language[15] which we have seen so bril-

[14] "Welles on Falstaff," *Cahier du Cinema in English*, No. 11 (1967), p. 7.

[15] "Familiar discourse" was a vital, new and at least secondary definition for "conversation" (dating from 1580, O.E.D.); its earlier

liantly displayed in Part 1 when Hal and Falstaff joined
to verbally disport themselves as Satirist. "Justice" sends
Falstaff and crew to prison in an act unjust even by accepted standards of monarchical executive power, since
Hal has just promised them maintenance and possible ad-
vancement even as he cut formal ties with them. The
bitterness of this conclusion rests on the revealed empti-
ness of the concept of Justice to which the young king
has pledged himself and on which most civilized societies
are based.

During the course of the play Falstaff's continual function is to expose through verbal attack the vacuity of the
established system of values. Although his symbiotic
relationship with Hal has lapsed into dormancy, until the
very end he speaks under the assumption that their ties
will not break with the stress of war. And Shakespeare
brings each of them on stage in a continued series of
paralleled and interrelated performances. Act I shows
how Falstaff, though part of the royal army, works with
his wit as a rebel against established values. From our
point of interest, the strategic part of Act II is the reaffir-
mation of the existence of the Falstaff-Hal Satirist, in
spite of great internal conflict. Act III provides the ideo-
logical support for the rebel Satirist's position. Act IV
arouses our hopes that, through Hal, the Establishment
will embrace this ill-fated rebel element—i.e., that dramatized social change will cause a satiric catharsis to sup-
plement the simpler comic release of the tavern scenes.

---

meaning of "behavior" or "social intercourse" was already old in
Shakespeare's time but is also applicable here; a possible third
level to the charge against Falstaff lies in the sixteenth-century use
of "conversation" to mean illicit sexual intercourse.

These hopes are not finally throttled, this purgation not definitively blocked, until the play's very last scene.

In going back to Act I now I will fill out this summary in such a way as to substantiate the theory for a correct production of the play based on its satiric plot.

The prologue to Part 2 is spoken by "Rumour, painted full of tongues" and makes the play's first thematic statement about the powerful deceptivity of speech, the unreliability of report, the whole rotting, shifty framework of the depicted world. Hotspur has been killed, yet Hal and his father are rumored dead: the result is that rebellion mysteriously rages on

Whiles the big year, swol'n with some other grief,
Is thought with child by the stern tyrant War.

(13–14)

In scene ii Falstaff begins to expose the quality of this "other grief."

As if from the Oedipus-like kingly source, all kinds of infection plague the kingdom. The satiric exposer, in spite of his perceptivity, is not exempt. In fact, in this interpretation, he becomes a paradigm for the nation's dis-ease. As the scene begins Falstaff's new page jests about the doctor's report on his master's physical condition. Falstaff takes the judgment as a taunt and brags about his own superior satiric wit—

> The brain of this foolish-compounded clay, man, is not able to invent anything that intends to laughter, more than I invent or is invented on me. I am not only witty in myself, but the cause that wit is in other men.

(I, ii, 8–12)

In the vanity of his supposed new affluence he rails at the page and at the prince who has favored him. When the page reminds him of his actually degenerate financial condition, Falstaff merely satirizes the merchant who asked for "security" before providing satin for new suits. In this speech, Falstaff bullishly rails against the economic system by incantationally repeating the word "security" five times in fifteen lines of witty prose.

In the rest of the scene, his dogged resistance to the Lord Chief Justice broadens his attack to include the accepted legal and moral systems of the age. After pretending deafness to the Chief Justice's call, Falstaff reverses his technique and mocks the nobleman with the reiteration of an exaggerated respect for his station:

> My good lord! God give your lordship good time of day! I am glad to see your lordship abroad. I heard say your lordship was sick. I hope your lordship goes abroad by advice. Your lordship, though not clean past your youth, hath yet some smack of age in you, some relish of the saltness of time; and I most humbly beseech your lordship to have a reverend care of your health.
>
> (106–114)

He makes a terse response to these ironically couched insults, these suggestions of the insidious senility of power. But Falstaff goes on impudently to discuss the king's apoplexy, which he describes as "a whoreson tingling." The nobleman flares at such a presumption; the inviolability of the king is the foundation of the system of justice he represents. By taking up the justice's metaphors and turning his sentences inside-out, Falstaff further undermines his sense of power and prevents him from making any convincing moral accusations against the spendthrift knight. So much headway does Falstaff make with his wit, that he can repudiate the justice's accusation of his being the prince's ill-angel with the following attack on the general morality of the age:

> Not so, my lord. Your ill angel is light, but I hope he that looks upon me will take me without weighing. And yet, in some respects, I grant, I cannot go. I cannot tell. Virtue is of so little regard in these costermonger's times that true valour is turn'd berod; pregnancy is made a tapster, and his quick wit wasted in giving reckonings. All the other gifts appertinent to man, as the malice of this age shapes them, are not worth a gooseberry.
>
> (187–196)

At the end of the encounter, Falstaff gets away very easily with his impudent request for a 1000–pound loan from the very official who came to accuse him of misappropriation of state funds.

If on the stage Falstaff were acted as a mere clown the satiric challenge and bite of his intricate speeches would be lost. He is not Hal's fool, but a vital component of the prince's intellectual life. Their protracted encounter in II, iv reaffirms the pull Falstaff has on Hal in spite of his resolutions to resist such unprincely influences. This entire act is devoted to the manifestations of resistance to duty: (i) Falstaff dodging his debts to Hostess Quickly, (ii) Hal desiring "small beer" when princely strength is called for,[16] (iii) wife and daughter trying to keep North-

[16] Erich Auerbach, *Mimesis*, trans. Willard R. Trask (1957), ch.

umberland back from battle, and (iv) the long interlude
at the Boarshead. This last scene includes many varieties
of satire as well as featuring satire as the subject of an
important discussion between the symbiotic satirists.

The first half of the scene shows satire as play with the
simple release accorded by good-natured imitative mockery in a detached context. Doll and Falstaff "pox" and
"hang" each other; Doll calls Pistol an assortment of
nasty names; Pistol parodies contemporary dramatic rant
and heroic rhetoric. But when the prince and Poins enter
in disguise, stage rear (231), Falstaff's language takes on
a sudden moral weight after the uproarious saturnalia
of the Pistol episode. Doll curiously begins to talk about
the prince (is she in on the trick?) in the suddenly serious
context of Falstaff's death: "What humour's the Prince
of?" Falstaff declares roundly,

> A good shallow young fellow. 'A would have made
> a good pantler; 'a would 'a chipp'd bread well.
>
> (256–258)

and goes on to call Poins a baboon with no more wit than
a mallet. The disguised pair quietly rail, in response,
about Falstaff's age and unseemly lovemaking. When he
calls "Francis" for some sack, and Poins and Hal answer,
"Anon, anon, sir," the quick-witted Falstaff, evidently
recognizing their voices, rallies to the trickery with, "Ha!
a bastard son of the King's?"

The prince now reverts to his hard moralistic line.
"Why, thou globe of sinful continents, what a life dost

13, uses this passage to discuss the mixture of styles in Shakespeare as evidenced in the prince's own duality of character and
speech.

thou lead!"—only to be rebuked, "A better than thou.
I am a gentleman; thou art a drawer." What, after all, is
the heir apparent doing dressed as a poor apprentice if
there is not some truth to the scandalous suggestion that
he is suited for pantry work? As the disguise comes off
in a rage, Falstaff has the further audacity to say, "Thou
whoreson mad compound of majesty, thou are welcome."
It is at this point that Poins warns the absolutist satirist
prince of the cathartic powers of Falstaff's wit:

> My lord, he will drive you out of your revenge, and
> turn all to a merriment, if you take not the heat.
>
> (323–325)

The prince has evidently been momentarily charmed
by the brazenly witty man and his affectionate Doll. But
he now takes up the moral line again and accuses Falstaff
of "speaking vilely" of him. Hal is most offended by the
thought that Falstaff recognized him all along ("as you
did when you ran away by Gadshill") and was engaged
in "wilful abuse," a serious offense. Five times Falstaff
excitedly denies being guilty of satire with malicious intent before he frames the clever disavowal,

> I disprais'd him before the wicked, that the wicked
> might not fall in love with him; in the which doing,
> I have done the part of a careful friend and a true
> subject, and thy father is to give me thanks for it.
> No abuse, Hal.
>
> (346–350)

This witty version of the satirist's traditional claim of
constructive, moral intent for his seemingly destructive

and irreverent attacks finally works—but only after Falstaff backs it up by showing the universality of "wickedness" and thereby implying its meaninglessness as a basis for judgment. Falstaff thus argues his way out of the trap with pseudo-moralistic rhetoric, and then destroys the moralistic position. When Hal is about to accuse the hostess of violation of Lenten dietary laws, skeptic Falstaff puts in the last word: "His grace says that which his flesh rebels against." Hal, like most people, has eaten flesh in Lent (probably served by this very Hostess) and is equally as "sinful" as any tavern habitué.

Act III further enforces the Falstaffian skeptical antivalues in two very different meditative speeches. Ailing King Henry's opening speech which ends, "uneasy lies the head that wears a crown," follows Falstaff's carefree and lusty night in the tavern to corroborate by dramatic contrast the natural, human, nonchivalric beliefs he stands for. The second scene, though it is the conscription of Mouldy, Shadow, Wart, Feeble and Bullcalf, contains little explicit satire. The conclusions all come in Falstaff's final soliloquy in which he reveals the extent of Justice Shallow's absurd lies. But the tone of the speech is meditative instead of satiric now that Falstaff is out of touch with his "other half" in satire, Hal. Falstaff always includes himself in moral exposé: "Lord, Lord, how subject we old men are to this vice of lying!" And by recruiting the worst of the ragged lot and vowing to fleece the lying "justice" he acts in accord with his previously only verbalized satiric stance against the Establishment.

The fourth act begins with the thematic statement of the ailing realm, phrased in terms of a purgation that is appropriate both to the diseased state metaphor and the

aesthetic catharsis under way. The Archbishop of York
justifies his part in the rebellion:

> . . . *we are all diseas'd*
> *And with our surfeiting and wanton hours*
> *Have brought ourselves into a burning fever,*
> *And we must bleed for it; of which disease*
> *Our late King, Richard, being infected, died . . .*
> *I take not on me here as a physician; . . .*
> *But rather show awhile like fearful war*
> *To diet rank minds, sick of happiness,*
> *And purge th'obstructions which begin to stop*
> *Our very veins of life.*

> (54–66)

The literal blood-letting of war is thus set up as purge
for the country and for the drama.

But quite in contrast to the climactic (though undercut) combat between Hal and Hotspur in Part 1, here,
even the blood-letting of battle is frustrated, dispersed
and made absurd.[17] In the second scene Westmoreland
and Prince John ignobly trick their enemy into a truce,
drink pledges over their promises, and then, when the
enemy army disbands, vilely arrest Hastings, the archbishop and Mowbray, in the name of God, for treacherous
rebellion.

What Shakespeare thinks of such behavior is made
quite clear when Falstaff comes on (in IV, iii) with his
parodically courtly capture of Coleville without a fight.

[17] Burckhardt, p. 149, says Part 1 (V, iii) provides that "discharge of tension which of itself seems to create a sense of order";
he posits the notion of "complementarity" (p. 185)—the simul-
taneous use of two different models—to explain the disparities of
the trilogy.

Prince John scolds Falstaff for such "tardy tricks" when
"everything is ended." But Falstaff's speech on valor
mocks the diplomatic "valour" we have recently witnessed in John's so-called victory:

> I never knew yet but rebuke and check was the re-
> ward of valour. . . . I have speeded hither with the
> very extremest inch of possibility; I have found'red
> ninescore and odd posts; and here, travel-tainted as
> I am, have, in my pure and immaculate valour, taken
> Sir John Coleville of the Dale, a most furious knight
> and valorous enemy. But what of that? He saw me,
> and yielded; that I may justly say with the hook-
> nosed fellow of Rome—I came, saw, and overcame.
> (35–46)

The Falstaff soliloquy on sherris sack (IV, iii, 91–135)
that follows contrasts Princes John and Henry. John has
no wit and no true "valour" for "valour" comes from
drink (which Falstaff proves in a burlesque of the humor
theory of medicine) and Hal is valiant because he has
tempered his father's cold blood with (Falstaff's) hot
wine. In the next scene King Henry's empty moralizing
on youthful valor quickly changes to bitterness when he
learns Hal is back in London with his old pals. Falstaff
seems to retain his hold on Hal: the crown scene (IV, iv),
for example, should be interpreted as further proof of
Hal's inherent "sherris sack" impetuosity; it is the Falstaffian brand of "valour" that prompts him to steal the
crown from the sleeping king, and the Falstaffian skill
in language that enables him to beautifully lie about his
motives in doing so. Thus Shakespeare builds up the Falstaffian disruptive force before he breaks it.

The irony of "justice" that pervades act V soon enough makes clear that Falstaffian satire has no place in the politics of a conventionally secure kingdom. In the first scene Falstaff looks forward to amusing Hal with his mocking judgments of such dignitaries as the foolish Justice Shallow. In the very next one, the Lord Chief Justice warns the new king about political chaos—by asking him to imagine now having a son like the hitherto unruly Prince Hal—

> To pluck down justice from your awful bench,
> To trip the course of law, and blunt the sword
> That guards the peace and safety of your person.

> (85–88)

With this speech he reverses Hal's enmity toward him (and the world he represents) and explicitly makes the young king adopt him as father figure. Hal even quotes the pious language of his dead father as he accredits the old line of legal power, the traditional, unreformed system of justice. Political security is dependent on the repudiation of all human values and the support of the conventional political machine with its unreal precepts of justice—as flawed and empty as they may be.

The irony of this decision comes through with the full depiction of those human values as embodied in the rejected Falstaff. In scene iii he is joyous at Hal's kingship and fully expects to profit from his connection, especially by having the Chief Justice soundly repudiated. But the hand of justice extends in scene iv to the seemingly harmless Doll and Hostess who are rudely arrested, and Falstaff's fall comes at the very height of his expectations when the king's procession passes in scene v. When Fal-

staff calls, "My sweet boy! my King! my Jove!" the now
starkly nonsatiric moralist replies:

> *I know thee not, old man. Fall to thy prayers.*
> *How ill white hairs become a fool and jester!*
> *I have long dreamt of such a kind of man,*
> *So surfeit-swell'd, so old, and so profane;*
> *But being awak'd, I do despise my dream.*
> *Make less thy body, hence, and more thy grace;*
> *Leave gormandizing. Know the grace doth gape*
> *For thee thrice wider than for other men.*
> *Reply not to me with a fool-born jest.*
> *Presume not that I am the thing I was;*
> *For God doth know (so shall the world perceive)*
> *That I have turn'd away my former self;*
> *So will I those that kept me company.*

The epilogue speaks of this having been "a displeasing
play." If the director heeds the satiric plot, as outlined
here, that is precisely the proper effect of the drama. The
uncomfortable feeling of displeasure comes from the
blocking of that satiric catharsis which would purge the
audience of emotions aroused to rebel against a hypo-
critically pious, evil and unjust government.

Falstaff must be presented with depth and serious-
ness; emphatic attention to detail must illuminate every
point of the Falstaffian philosophy. Yet his particular
character should not be romanticized to such a degree
that he is raised to tragic levels. The end does not depict
the "Death of a Salesman," but the rejection of a satiric
rebel. Hal's turnabout in the final scene thus ends the
play with biting irony precisely because Falstaff is *not*

a Scapegoat[18] like Jaques of *As You Like It*: England in the play is no Arden, and rather than bear away all societal discord and evil, Falstaff makes us painfully aware of its pervasion of the entire world.

Unlike the ending of Part 1, the satiric "curse," i.e., the witty criticism, is frustrated, prevented from "working" by Hal's sudden rejection of Falstaff and his turning toward the standard bearers of unreformed traditional values. The rejection has an unsettling effect on the audience[19] because it abruptly stops the hitherto effective playing out of satiric aggressions. Because the brand of hatred and censure that has been stirred up by Falstaffian satire is denied final outlet on stage, the audience should come back into Elizabethan society (or any society) with the bitter taste of satire still on their tongues and the exposing satiric light in their eyes.

[18] Cesar Lombardi Barber, "Saturnalia in the Henriad," in *Shakespeare: Modern Essays in Criticism* (1961), p. 176, taking a ritualistic instead of an aesthetic point of view, concludes that Falstaff is the Misrule Scapegoat with his speech on honor reminiscent of the primitive scapegoat's presacrifice speech; in this view *1 Henry IV* is analogous to the Saturnalian reign of Carnival (eating and drinking emphasized for holiday motif) and *2 Henry IV* is likened to Carnival on Trial, in which the scapegoat is run out of town as a folk custom way of "limiting, by ritual, the attitudes and impulses set loose by ritual" (p. 182).

[19] Welsford, p. 281, compares the rejection of Falstaff to the death of Calderon's clown in *Life Is A Dream* by a stray shot: "The two dramatists are at one in their abrupt repudiation of this type of fool, and their declaration in favour of the moral law which it is his whole business to evade. Yet their remorselessness affects us disagreeably. The fool is our champion against the facts of life and the fact of death. He should surely at least be victorious in imaginative literature. But perhaps Calderon and Shakespeare are right. The seers who know that life is a dream are never sentimental."

Enid Welsford believes the Falstaffian type of clownage to act as a

> social preservative by providing a corrective to the pretentious vanity of officialdom, a safety-valve for unruliness, a wholesome nourishment to the sense of secret spiritual independence of that which would otherwise be the intolerable tyranny of circumstance.
>
> (p. 317)

But we must remember that Falstaff is more than a clown or standard fool. Miss Welsford goes on to contrast the emancipatory effect of "birth of new joy or freedom" coming from the fool in jest with the purpose of the "revolutionary in earnest":

> The latter may change the system . . . but he can do nothing to protect, and is indeed far more likely to attack, that individual spiritual integrity which the social group did not give and the social group cannot take away.
>
> (p. 319)

The symbiotic satirist of the *Henry IV* plays teeters between the fool and the revolutionary; on the whole he is allowed free play in Part 1 as the fool who cures through catharsis but is finally rejected in Part 2 when his revolutionary effect overtakes that of clownage.

The text, then, dictates that 2 *Henry IV*, because its ending displeases, should provoke discontent with established rule and courtly values, thus exemplifying Plato's fears about the effects of art on society. But the equilibrium of interpretation necessary for such a production has proven difficult to achieve. It is much easier for the director to present an uproarious comedy, or even a heartrending tragedy, than the delicately balanced satiric drama that Shakespeare wrote.

4: Jaques: The Pharmakos
Railer of Comedy

SEVERAL KEY SCENES in *As You Like It* show how a
satirist works in a clearly comic world. In this play
satiric catharsis results from the important presence of
the melancholic scapegoat in comedy's world of otherwise
harmonious resolutions. This chapter's three sections correspond to three different parts of the play. Key scene
for the theorizing about satiric catharsis is II, vii. Key
scene for the practical demonstration of various kinds of
satire and their effects is III, ii. The aesthetic mechanism
of rejection leading to catharsis begins notably with IV,
i and pervades most of the last act.

The second act of the play belongs to Jaques. After
devoting most of it to building him up as the traditional
satirist-railer, in scene vii Shakespeare makes explicit
the question of Jaques's role in the satiric catharsis of
the play. Jaques's fascination with Touchstone is based
on his preoccupation with the possible interplay between
cathartic laughter and effective satire.

Our introduction to Jaques comes in the form of an
expository scene (II, i) in which he is described as a man
of sensibility who weeps over a wounded deer. In an age

of teeming forests this may have indicated an unbalanced disposition, undoubtedly with some affliction of the humors, but in itself by no means conveys an unsympathetic or absurd portrait. Indeed, we are told that Jaques is of a contemplative nature and "moralized" about the deer (44). Like the Roman satirists he "most invectively" pierced "through the body of the country, city court" (58) in his anger at the other unpitying animals and the men who defile the forests. Duke Senior, living and hunting merrily in Arden, is anxious to find Jaques in this "sullen" mood, "For then he's full of matter." The duke highly values the disputatious nature of a satirist in this sylvan society.

In case there is still any doubt that Jaques represents the traditional satirist,[1] Shakespeare portrays him in scene V as a melancholic[2] who is sarcastic, insulting and gifted in occult poetry. After railing at the singer and criticizing the duke, he recites a verse he has written which surely satirizes the duke:

---

[1] Sujata Chaudhuri, "Shakespeare and the Elizabethan Satire Tradition," *Shakespeare Commemoration Volume* (1966), p. 172, selects Jaques as the most representative of all Shakespeare's satirists: "Into his mouth Shakespeare puts words which are expressive of exactly the same attitude as had been taken up by the formal verse satirists of Elizabethan England."

[2] Theodore Spencer, "The Elizabethan Malcontent," *Joseph Quincy Adams Memorial Studies* (1948), p. 528, finds that Jaques (like Hamlet) has a trace of the "diseased melancholy" in him, though neither is a medical case. The misanthropic malcontent (Jaques, Thersites, Timon, Apemantus) is a type of the larger category of Melancholy. Spencer's "malcontent type number 5" (from Renaissance medical tracts) best fits Jaques: this is the "satirical ranter who is congenitally outside of society, not displaced by a particular set of circumstances" (p. 530).

> *If it do come to pass*
> *That any man turn ass,*
> *Leaving his wealth and ease*
> *A stubborn will to please,*
> *Ducdame, ducdame, ducdame!*
> *Here shall he see*
> *Gross fools as he,*
> *An if he will come to me.*
>
> (II, v, 52–59)

The "stubborn will" would refer to Duke Frederick who was allowed to usurp his brother's lands and title. Jaques explains the refrain "ducdame" as "a Greek invocation to call fools into a circle"—perhaps a lighthearted allusion to Greek iambic curse incantations or word magic. To complete his satirist's credentials, Jaques refers with his exit line to the railing Herod of the English mystery play: "I'll go sleep, if I can; if I cannot, I'll rail against all the first-born of Egypt." Railing here reaches back to its origin in killing.

The duke is inclined to treat Jaques as a kind of court fool in the forest, but the fool's role is not native to the melancholic misanthrope.[3] The only joy Jaques shows throughout the play relates to his discovery of the court fool proper, Touchstone, with the possibility this new role holds out to him for integrating his dissonant satiric inclinations with society. He enters scene vii full of enthusiasm about Touchstone: "A fool, a fool! I met a fool

[3] Robert Harris Goldsmith, *Wise Fools in Shakespeare* (1963), p. 68, says that such characters as Jaques are satiric commentators, not wise fools like Touchstone, and their urge to speak invective comes from "a genuine or affected melancholy humour or from mere envy at the good fortune of others."

i' th' forest, / A motley fool!" He quotes the fool's little speech on "how the world wags" which made him laugh for an hour "That fools should be so deep contemplative." He is struck by Touchstone's similarity to himself, in that both are railing critics, but is envious of the motley coat (official costume of the Renaissance fool) which gives one the license to satirize without risking the loss of one's place in society:

> *It is my only suit,*
> *Provided that you weed your better judgments*
> *Of all opinion that grows rank in them*
> *That I am wise. I must have liberty*
> *Withal, as large a charter as the wind,*
> *To blow on whom I please; for so fools have.*
> *And they that are most galled with my folly,*
> *They most must laugh.*
>
>   (II, vi, 44–51)

Behind this speech lies one interpretation of the mechanism of satiric catharsis: Jaques is noting that a release of laughter in the "victim" inevitably follows the fool's satiric attacks. This can be the only reasonable reaction because it would be high folly to strike back at a fool (51–55).

"Invest me in my motley" says the extraordinarily enthusiastic Jaques: he wants to become a simple fool who releases laughter. But his next speech, using a medical figure popular for the subject,[4] evokes a different aspect of satiric catharsis:

---

[4] Mary Claire Randolph, "The Medical Concept in English Renaissance Satiric Theory" (1941), p. 145: "So speak all the various types of satirically minded malcontents, quasi-malcontents, professional railers, and their kind."

> *Give me leave*
> *To speak my mind, and I will through and through*
> *Cleanse the foul body of the infected world,*
> *If they will patiently receive my medicine.*
>
> (58–61)

Here Jaques reverts to the traditionally moralistic line of
the satirist and looks to the curative power of his attacks
to purge the disease of evil from his victims. Thus he
seizes on the new disguise of motley as a possible means
of effecting a seemingly incompatible merger of pur-
poses. As a serious satirist dressed in a fool's costume
he hopes to actually cure his society by verbally attacking
its sins and sinners without suffering the retaliatory
castigation usual for the satirist. He in fact hopes to
receive payment in laughter for his medico-moral services.

The duke's immediate response gives the first hint of
the illusory quality of Jaques's hopes. The satirist fully
expects to "do but good" (63), but the hitherto friendly
duke retorts,

> *Most mischievous foul sin, in chiding sin.*
> *For thou thyself hast been a libertine,*
> *As sensual as the brutish sting itself;*
> *And all th' embossed sores and headed evils*
> *That thou with license of free foot hast caught,*
> *Wouldst thou disgorge into the general world.*
>
> (64–69)

As Miss Randolph points out, the duke here is accusing
Jaques of being in reality more concerned with a personal
catharsis than with a curative catharsis. The implied
charge that the satirist's own corruption makes him unsuited to cast stones has its roots in the Latin satirists'

confession of an inner fury seeking a necessary outlet:[5]
with the Renaissance predilection for medical metaphor
in satiric theory, this force was said then to come from
pent up, diseased humors characteristic of the saturnine
character (by which Thomas Drant in 1566 linked "satyre" and "Saturn" in an erroneous etymology[6]). The
idea of the melancholy satirist as a "sick" person, then,
did not wait for the modern psychoanalyst[7] to come into
being; it sprang naturally from the tradition and from the
particular interests of the age.[8]

The moral difficulty of fooling with fooling thus immediately blocks Jaques's resolution. There is a basic
conflict between the fool's motley and Saturn's black.
But Jaques rallies to the duke's charge with a set speech
from the formal satirists on the pervasiveness of evil
among all men:

[5] See Chapter I above and Randolph, p. 154, n. 67.

[6] Randolph, pp. 150–152: "Of all planets the most malignant
and most baleful with the greatest power for evil and the spread
of incurable diseases," Saturn also figured "as the patron power of
satirists because he had overwhelming destructive forces at his
command" and provided "a February face and a gloomy disposition"; thought to be the planet farthest from the sun, its black
sign was expected to bequeath a chill aridity; "Blackness and
frigidity . . . have been satire's very own color and quality from
the Celtic hilltop satire, which demanded a cold black wind blowing, to Hegelian analyses of satiric aridity and objective 'distance'."
For Saturn as the star of Melancholy, see Raymond Klibansky,
Erwin Panofsky and Fritz Saxl, *Saturn and Melancholy* (1964), pp.
127–214—a major book on the subject.

[7] Isador H. Coriat, "The Psychology of Medical Satire," *Annals
of Medical History* (1921), pp. 403–407, passim.

[8] John D. Peter, *Complaint and Satire in Early English Literature* (1956), p. 204, believes that the satirist had turned backbiter
by 1600 and "was in a much more equivocal position, and the very
thoroughness with which he had turned backbiter made nonsense
of his protestations of rectitude."

Why, who cries out on pride
That can therein tax any private party?
Doth it not flow as hugely as the sea
Till that the wearer's very means do ebb?
What woman in the city do I name
When that I say the city woman bears
The cost of princes on unworthy shoulders?
Who can come in and say that I mean her,
When such a one as she, such is her neighbor?
Or what is he of basest function
That says his bravery is not on my cost,
Thinking that I mean him, but therein suits
His folly to the mettle of my speech?
There then! how then? what then? Let me see wherein
My tongue hath wronged him. If it do him right,
Then he hath wronged himself. If he be free,
Why, then my taxing like a wild goose flies,
Unclaimed of any man.

(70–87)

Thus Jaques ends his flirtation with motley by reverting
strongly to his habitual mode as caustic satirist.

That he cannot, in spite of his fascination, play the
fool, is nowhere better illustrated than at the end of
this very scene with his "All the world's a stage" speech.
The discussion of the satirist's function in society was
interrupted after Jaques's defense by the abrupt appearance of Orlando seeking sustenance for his starving servant. When Orlando goes to bring old Adam to the feast,
leaving the duke and most of his men touched with the
"woeful pageant" of his distress, Jaques opens out with
his best and most sweepingly satiric speech. As satirist
he is inclined to bitterly mock Orlando's romantic de-

meanor and sentimental reference to Adam as his "poor
fallen fawn." Jaques's tirade on the seven ages of man
is the acrid, satiric version of Touchstone's merry time-
telling of "how the world wags" which Jaques admired
enough to quote earlier. In contrast to the fool's, the satirist's speech is loaded with the ammunition of realistic
imagery.

It is also backed up by such ugly realities as the malice
of Oliver and Duke Frederick in act I and by the direct
social criticism[9] which precedes Jaques's attack. Speaking
to old Adam, Orlando mourns the passing of the "an-
tique world":

> *Thou art not for the fashion of these times,*
> *Where none do sweat but for promotion,*
>
> (II, iii, 59–60)

and Corin reveals the antipastoral realities of the shepherd's life:

> *I am shepherd to another man*
> *And do not shear the fleeces that I graze.*
> *My master is of churlish disposition . . .*
>
> (II, iv, 77–80)

But Shakespeare foreshadows the ineffectiveness of satiric
criticism in this play's world when he follows Jaques's

[9] This social criticism of "France" and "Arden" had ample in-
spiration in the real world of the late sixteenth century. The failure
of seven harvests, famine and plague in 1592, setbacks in trade
and low purchasing power of wages added social unrest to the
general political stagnation; one result was the appearance of the
angry young men of the 1590s, the University Wits, who con-
tributed to the satirical expressions of the period. See Bernard
Harris, "Dissent and Satire," *Shakespeare in His Own Age: Shakespeare Survey* (1964) pp. 129–130.

brilliant speech with the unshakenly sentimental reception of Orlando and Adam which ends act II. Only the
"Most friendship is feigning, most loving mere folly"
line in Amiens's song even acknowledges Jaques's attack
on the dignity of human life.

Act III, scene ii of the play provides, almost in pageant
fashion, examples of how the differing cathartic and noncathartic satirists work in the forest of Arden. In addition
to Touchstone's non-sensical laugh purges and the con-
trasting noncathartic satire of Jaques we have the playfully cathartic wit of Rosalynd.

As Enid Welsford notes, the controversial spirit of the
Renaissance often looked to the fool as an effective and
comparatively safe mouthpiece for the utterance of political discontent.[10] In our scene, the fool directs attacks
at the shepherd Corin and at Rosalynd in order to criticize the social and literary temper of the times, but his
style is a typically "safe" one:

> Even when he speaks as a satirist, the fool prefers to make his
> comments by indirection. He voices his criticism by innuendo,
> parody, and the apposite recitation of old songs.[11]

Touchstone's mock rationalistic attack on country life—

> Why, if thou never wast at court, thou never saw'st
> good manners; if thou never saw'st good manners,
> then thy manners must be wicked; and wickedness
> is sin, and sin is damnation. Thou art in a parlous
> state, shepherd.
>
>   (41–45)

[10] *The Fool* (1961), p. 141.
[11] Goldsmith, p. 78.

—must really be completely inverted to yield up its criticism of court manners, morals and rhetoric. This kind of satire, like the verbally intricate merriment of Falstaff's tavern satire, is far too oblique and satisfyingly witty in itself to actually cleanse any worldly infection.

When he turns his skills to a slightly more direct criticism of courtly life through the doggerel parody of Orlando's love lyric, Touchstone's attack is immediately rejected by Rosalynd's "Peace you dull fool!" (as well as by the audience's laughter). The recitation of verses is part of the fool's social function; when he attempts to be a satirist-physician by asking why Rosalynd "infects" herself (line 120) with bad verses, he is only forced to fulfill the rest of his function as fool and be rebuked by her aroused wit. For many more lines after Touchstone's exit, Rosalynd and Celia make merry over those absurdities in the verses which he had pointed out. The fool allows for the release of socially repressed emotions through laughter. The exposure of Orlando's sentimental absurdities and low literary taste in no way prevents Rosalynd from admiring and then marrying him. To be sure, masquerading as Ganymede, she later manages to have some fun at Orlando's expense, but in doing so, she merely purges that discordant wit which might have marred the love resolutions of Arden's comic world.

Rosalynd's playfully cathartic satire is further illustrated later in the scene when Shakespeare makes her the merry mouthpiece for more of the play's social criticism. Since the occasion is in fact her first encounter with Orlando in her male disguise, it is no surprise that she feels something of the ancient satyr's freedom to criticize.[12] Like Touchstone and Jaques, she begins with a

[12] See the beginning of Chapter III, above.

witty speech on Time (326 ff). In it she names some of
the more notable characters of her age: the Latin-less
priest, the gouty rich man, and the lethargic lawyer—all
traditional subjects for satiric attack. But the magical
power of satire is lacking in Rosalynd's comments. She
has wit and acute perceptivity but none of the anger or
hatred that traditionally drive the satirist; her bite lacks
the fangs of curse.[13] The dramatic situation of course dictates this since her flamboyance only results from the
playful mood imposed by her disguise. Her entire "cure"
of Orlando's love sickness (385 ff) is also only a pretense
which permits her to expound mockingly on the lean
cheek, etc. of the typically lovesick youth; she does not
intend actually to cure him through mockery. The whole
Ganymede courting motif then becomes a laugh purge
and a spoof on satire as cure because the lady actually
wants her man madly in love and finally "cures" him not
with burlesque but with reality—herself in a gown.

Jaques appears in our parade scene of satirists-in-action
between Touchstone and Rosalynd. His language and
effects contrast sharply with theirs. He enters (line 266)
railing directly at Orlando (whereas Touchstone had
used the indirection of parody and Rosalynd that of her
disguise): "I pray you mar no more trees with writing love
songs in their barks." He flatly criticizes Rosalynd's
name and in order to attack Orlando's sentimentality
makes insinuations about his former acquaintance with
"goldsmiths' wives" (line 288). When Jaques invites Orlando to rail with him "against our mistress the world
and all our misery," he refuses, being too honestly self-

---

[13] Just as later (III, v) she shows the moralistic bent of the
satirist in her long, somewhat angry speech to Phebe, but lacks
the magical component of satire's characteristic language.

critical and not of the same complaining nature as this "Monsieur Melancholy." But the satirist's provocative presence seems to sharpen the tongue even of an Orlando, and, with considerable spirit, he gets rid of Jaques by shooting a few quick insults at him.

In all of this Jaques remains the true satirist, even though early in the play he takes a nearly defeated position. Except for his jewel-like Seven Ages of Man speech, he usually contents himself with brief, derogatory remarks that rail but never build to the power of the satiric spell. In III, iii, Jaques provides the satiric chorus of asides to the "courting" scene between Touchstone and Audrey. He mocks Touchstone's reference to Ovid and the Goths: "O knowledge ill-inhabited, worse than Jove in a thatch'd house!" (11). He debunks the fool as "material" (32) when Touchstone uses a homely maxim. He is sarcastic (46). All of this he delivers in incantation-like asides. Coming forward, he then becomes much more moral and makes caustic comments on the perils of marriage.

> Get you to church, and have a good priest that can tell you what marriage is. This fellow will but join you together as they join wainscot; then one of you will prove a shrunk panel, and like green timber warp, warp.
>
> (86–90)

Thus, in act III, while Jaques tries in vain to cleanse the foul body of the infected world with his satire, the more light-hearted satiric commentators whom he had so admired in theory (II, vii) are free to blow on whom they please because in so doing they raise only the storm of laughter.

From act IV on, the rejection of the satirist gains momentum until his final expulsion in the last, otherwise harmonious, scene. Satirizing the satirist becomes the prime purpose of Rosalynd's one exchange with Jaques (IV, i, 1–38), since she here reveals him as the typical Malcontent Traveler of the day who affected Italianate manners, disdained his own country, dressed in black, was solitary, changeable, bankrupt, and potentially dangerous because skilled in Italian fencing arts.[14] Rosalynd's good-natured mockery cuts into Jaques's life as a traveler:

> A traveller! By my faith you have great reason to be sad. I fear you have sold your own lands to see other men's. Then to have seen much and to have nothing is to have rich eyes and poor hands . . . Farewell, Monsieur Traveller. Look you lisp and wear strange suits, disable all the benefits of your own country, be out of love with your nativity and almost chide God for making you that countenance you are; or I will scarce think you have swam in a gundello.
>
> (21–25, 33–37)

With these speeches she verbally chases the satirist off-stage. He is able only to cast one last insult at Orlando (for speaking in blank verse). Thus the only time we laugh at Jaques on stage is when he is the subject of a

[14] Z. S. Fink, "Jaques and the Malcontent Traveler" (1935), p. 248, says that if Jaques were to act instead of rail, "he would, because of his corrupted nature, be a vicious and dangerous man."

well-aimed counterattack. Alvin Kernan describes the effect as follows:

Jaques, though he is used as a device for deflating the poses of the other characters, is satirized in turn, and the principal method by which he is attacked is caricature, the process of seizing on his more ridiculous attitudes and magnifying them to the point where they are patently laughable.[15]

By laughing at him we can release the energies of hatred and censure of society which his usual presence elicits, but release them back on the debunker himself, thus nullifying the critical value of his satire by reversing its emotional voltage.

Rosalynd's attack thus makes us feel we need not be overly affected by Jaques's pessimistic Seven Ages of Man speech, or by the real discord in the real world (indicated in acts I and II), because he after all is just a sick man, a new type of melancholic, laughably prey to the Italianate affectations of the moment and not worth our serious thought. Indeed, modern medicine classes melancholia with the psychoses, characterized by persistent antisocial behavior caused by the inability to love; the melancholic "can only hate, and cannot conform to the pattern of behaviour required by society."[16] This description, so applicable to the satirist in general (who, however, is not necessarily psychotic), merely revamps Renaissance "psychologists" on the subject: one of these tells us that excess of choler may be purged with wormwood, lentozic, violets, etc., but an excess of unnatural melancholy is a dangerous condition requiring the ser-

---

[15] Alvin B. Kernan, *The Cankered Muse* (1959), p. 132.
[16] William Inglis Dunn Scott, *Shakespeare's Melancholics* (1962), pp. 25 and 28.

vices of a physician (an "honest and perfect" one), for unnatural melancholy "Procedeth of the abustion of choleric mixture, and is hotter and lighter, having in it violence to kill, with a dangerous disposition."[17] Babb calls Jaques the best example of the melancholy malcontent in the role of philosophic critic, and the kindliest portrait of the type in Elizabethan and Stuart literature.[18] Indeed, in the very scene where his melancholy is mocked, he is able to defend it as being akin to that of the scholar, musician, courtier, soldier, lawyer, lady and lover (10–20)— thus anticipating Burton on the subject. His rejection is mitigated at this point because

Melancholy was rapidly becoming in 1600 a disillusion shared by the age, and shared, furthermore, by Shakespeare. A few years earlier, the melancholy and cynicism of the traveler had been material for satire and laughter, and they still were in 1600, but the laughter was becoming increasingly difficult.[19]

Nevertheless, Shakespeare must sacrifice the satirist in order to retain the comic integrity of a turn-of-the-century Arden. In act V he turns the satiric art of parody back on Jaques so that Touchstone and Rosalynd help us laugh the satirist's curses away. Touchstone belittles through laughter both ill-humor and satiric power in his parody of the satirist's curse, ostensibly directed against William, his lowly competitor in love. The pseudo-satirist declares that he will marry Audrey:

Therefore, you clown, abandon (which is in the vulgar, leave) the society (which in the boorish is,

[17] Sir Thomas Elyot, *The Castell of Helth* (1541), pp. 60A, 61B, 10B.

[18] Lawrence Babb, *The Elizabethan Malady* (1951), p. 93.

[19] Fink, p. 252.

company) of this female (which in the common is, woman); which together is, abandon the society of this female, or, clown, thou perishest; or, to thy better understanding, diest; or, to wit, I kill thee, make thee away, translate thy life into death, thy liberty into bondage. I will deal in poison with thee, or in bastinado, or in steel. I will bandy with thee in faction; I will o'errun thee with policy; I will kill thee a hundred and fifty ways. Therefore tremble and depart.

(V, i, 52–62)

The exaggerated piercing, poisoning, and killing (with all of the complicated rhetoric of real satire), though clearly threatened in a mood of high jest, proves effective when the "victim" immediately leaves. In the next scene, Rosalynd's claim to magical powers (she even conjures in the epilogue and refers to Irish rat-rhyming at III, ii, 187–188) further belittles the satiric claim to manipulate fates through preternatural means, since, of course, her magic is merely the trickery of her disguise. But she plays up her white magic (blessings) counterpoint to Jaques's black magic (curses) by the protracted series of dizzying promises made to Phebe, Orlando, Silvius and herself regarding their marriages.

At the beginning of the play's final scene (the comedy's resolution and a key scene for this study), Jaques and Touchstone each have a speech that is characteristic of them and of their satiric functions. As C. L. Barber has observed, the play's overall comic method is the reverse of satire, which usually presents life as it is and ridicules it for not being ideal; here we have ideal life, mocked because it does not square with ordinary life.[20] As pairs of matched lovers irrepressibly converge in the forest, Jaques limits his mockery to one pithy strike: "There is, sure, another flood toward, and these couples are coming to the ark" (35). He then must give the spotlight to Touchstone, the more congenial satirist. The fool's speeches on "quarrel" (71–86 and 93–108) please everyone present, especially the duke and Jaques (his impressario, as it were). Touchstone's extended performance provokes the peals of laughter which Jaques's brief lashing could not. Instead of attacking the actual people present, Touchstone criticizes general social rhetoric in his "quarrel" speeches in a highly stylized, oblique and witty manner that makes him a totally acceptable social satirist. While I do not agree with Barber that we laugh *at* and reject Touchstone, making him a scapegoat, it seems quite true that he does elicit from us a purgative laughter through which we deny our own ridiculousness.

The obvious evidence that Touchstone is not the play's scapegoat lies in the comic marriage resolution plot in which he participates, with Audrey, as a lover along with the rest. If his bride's indelicate behavior and his own cavalier attitude mockingly hint at the artificiality of Arden's harmony, they do so from within the main structure of the romantic plot instead of from the external vantage-point traditional to the true satirist. It has been said that satire "alienates itself from the objects of its scorn or derision, and it alienates us from them."[21] In

[20] Cesar Lombardi Barber, "The Use of Comedy in *As You Like It*," (1942), p. 356.

[21] Edgar Johnson, "Satiric Overtones in Shakespeare," *A Treasury of Satire* (1945), p. 156.

the play this distancing is the job not of the colorful Touchstone, but of the shadowy Jaques.

After Hymen has joined the various couples in a sylvan ceremony, Jaques takes note of the miraculous announcement that Duke Frederick has been suddenly converted from his evil ways to a religious life. The satirist declares himself "for other than for dancing measures" and prepares to join the duke in his philosophic cave. Helen Gardner notes that while Touchstone is the parodist who loves what he mocks, Jaques remains the uncontrovertable cynic.[22] She sees his function in terms of the elimination and nullification of the hatred that drives him:

A certain sour distaste for life is voided through him, something most of us feel at some time or other. If he were not there to give expression to it, we might be tempted to find the picture of life in the forest too sweet.

(p. 31)

This view accords with Frye's belief that the essence of the comic resolution is "an individual release which is also a social reconciliation."[23] Jaques exits to the cave of contemplation, bearing off with him those angry, contentious emotions which his satire, and that of the play's other ironists, has aroused. The social reconciliation remaining in Arden thus transmits an aesthetic harmony which leaves the audience satisfied instead of provoked.

Jaques's last speech is a toothless parody of Hymen's awarding of the nuptials. But it takes the most unsatiric form of the blessing, bequeathing well-deserved happiness to all—with the exception of Touchstone who has a

[22] Helen Gardner, "*As You Like It*," in *More Talking of Shakespeare*, John Garrett, ed. (1959), p. 29.

[23] Northrup Frye, "The Argument of Comedy" in *English Institute Essays*, D. A. Robertson, ed. (1948), p. 61.

future of wrangling for his "loving voyage is but for two
months victualled." Jaques had admired Touchstone's
skill and freedom as a satirist without fully realizing that
the freedom depended on the fool's integration with his
society. The cursing tone of Jaques's upsetting forecast
for him provides something of the rebuke usually the
everyday lot of the satirist; Touchstone has gotten away
freely until now with his criticism. But the punishment
is mild and far removed, for the celebratory masque begins, with Touchstone taking part, the moment the scapegoat satirist exits to bear off gloom. In the end, the play's
satire,

devoid of the venom distilled by human envy, is mollified to
harmonize with Shakespeare's characteristically humane spirit
of ridicule. It does not submerge the love story; it only gives
it the charm of psychic distance.[24]

But this is true only of the comedy as pure as *As You
Like It* and may be accepted only after acknowledging
the disruptive part played by its satire. It is the *pharmakos*
of satiric catharsis who makes the comedy the socially
pragmatic event that it is:

In promoting the mastery of passion by expression, dramatic
art can provide a civilized equivalent for exorcism. The exorcism represented as magically accomplished at the conclusion of the comedy is accomplished, in another sense, by the
whole dramatic action, as it keeps moving through release to
clarification.[25]

If pure comedy were all a dramatist such as Shakespeare
could invent as a literary vehicle for satire, art would be

[24] Oscar James Campbell, *Shakespeare's Satire* (1963), p. 63.
[25] Cesar Lombardi Barber, *Shakespeare's Festive Comedy* (1959),
p. 139.

a lot less troublesome and intriguing than it is. The critic
who flatly states, for example, that "Shakespeare is no
Juvenalian moralist scourging his characters with whips
of scorpions,"[26] has not taken account of the dramatist's
full range from satiric history through comedy to such a
pure satire as *Troilus and Cressida*—and even on to
satiric tragedy.

[26] Johnson, p. 156. Mrs. Chaudhuri also claims Shakespeare as
a mild Horatian.

5: Thersites and
Infectious Satire

In such unpopular plays as . . . Troilus
and Cressida *we find Shakespeare ready
and willing to start at the nineteenth century if the seventeenth would only let him.*
—SHAW

WHY THERSITES?

ONE OF THE very first puzzles in this enigmatic play is
the curious mentioning of the satirist Thersites at I, iii,
70–74, during the council of the Greeks, at a time when
he has no part in the dialogue or action and evidently has
not yet appeared on stage. Agamemnon's five-line speech
gratuitously referring to the snarling satirist does not
logically fit into the dialogue; it is syntactically crabbed
and semantically obscure.

The context of the puzzling lines is as follows: Ulysses
has just made a formal introduction to what will be his
big speech on Degree—the speech that has been taken to
represent the traditional concepts of the hierarchical
Elizabethan World Picture. To Ulysses' formal request
to be heard Agamemnon replies:

> *Speak, Prince of Ithaca; and be't of less expect*
> *That matter needless, of importless burthen,*
> *Divide thy lips than we are confident,*
> *When rank Thersites opes his mastic jaws,*
> *We shall hear music, wit, and oracle.*

If we assume this to be a normal, well-integrated Shake-spearean speech, we look for a clue to its meaning in the dialogue immediately following. But Ulysses replies:

> *Troy, yet upon his basis, had been down,*
> *And the great Hector's sword had lacked a master*
> *But for these instances:*
> *The specialty of rule hath been neglected; . . .*

and proceeds to blame the Greek "sickness" and the consequent stalemate in the war on the shaking of the ladder of degree caused by such willful warriors as the sulking Achilles.

In the earliest extant text of the play, the 1609 Quarto, Agamemnon's interruptive reference to Thersites is omitted. It appears only in the First Folio. William Rolfe paraphrases the difficult speech in the 1898 Harper edition: "There is less expectation of hearing needless and purposeless matter from you than confidence of hearing Thersites speak sweetly, wittily, or wisely."

If Shakespeare did write this odd little speech, he must have inserted it as a revision some time between 1609 and 1616; if he did not, an actor, editor or collaborator made the addition some time between 1609 and 1623. Either way, the speech indicates a greater stress on the character of Thersites by affording him a bit of an act I build-up. And it seems likely that if the lines were not actually composed by the author, they would at least have been added with his knowledge or at his suggestion after the first public airing of the play when it achieved its final form. The much debated question of if and where the play was performed (publicly at the Globe, or privately at an Inn of Court) cannot really be settled without further evidence. The play's first registration in 1603 claims it had already been acted but even if the play was only read, its first reception very likely caused enough of a stir so that later editions and/or performances were modified in various ways.

The title page of the first issue of the 1609 Quarto merely claims the play was "acted by the King's Majesties servants at the Globe." The same year this Quarto appeared in what may properly be called a second state with a cancel fold for the title page probably printed while the play was going through the presses.[1] The new title emphasizes the love of Troilus and Cressida and "the conceited wooing of Pandarus." It also includes an anonymous prose address to the reader that seems to imply the play had not been acted, or else not before a "vulgar" audience, and stresses its wit. The Folio text begins with a grim "armed prologue" (not appearing in Quarto) that emphasizes the war story and the bitter tone. To further our impression that the play underwent shifting interpretations, we note that it was originally registered as simply "Troilus and Cressida," is called a History in the first Quarto, but praised as a Comedy in the cancel fold preface; in First Folio it is entitled Tragedy but slipped in between the histories and tragedies (and in 1938 O. J. Campbell labeled it Comicall Satyre).

[1] W. W. Greg, ed., *Troilus and Cressida, First Quarto, 1609* (1951), intro., n.p.

The revision introducing Thersites helps to focus the play on the theme of the satirist. Although the lines are not well woven into the immediate dialogue, the subsequent references to satiric forces in the play make them appropriate and illuminate Ulysses' important speech on Degree. In his diagnosis and prescription for the Greek "illness" Ulysses describes Patroclus as, in effect, a kind of satirist—a scurrile jester, slanderer and "pageanter" who imitates other Greeks to ridicule them (I, iii, 140 ff). In order to finally accuse Achilles of the Greek failure Ulysses must work backward through the softening influence of Patroclus on the great warrior. Old Nestor, incensed at being one of the mocked targets of these loafing warriors' charades, helps pinpoint the cause of the societal infection:

> *And in the imitation of these twain—*
> *Who, as Ulysses says, opinion crowns*
> *With an imperial voice—many are infect:*
> *Ajax is grown self-will'd and bears his head*
> *In such a rein, in full as proud a place*
> *As broad Achilles; keeps his tent like him;*
> *Makes factious feasts; rails on our state of war,*
> *Bold as an oracle, and sets Thersites,*
> *A slave whose gall coins slanders like a mint,*
> *To match us in comparisons with dirt,*
> *To weaken and discredit our exposure,*
> *How rank soever rounded in with danger.*
>
> (I, iii, 185–196)

Agamemnon's Folio speech on Thersites clearly sets the railer at the head of a whole camp of disruptive satiric speakers.

The general's very compulsion to denigrate Thersites indicates the dangerous verbal power the satirist possesses. As Bertrand Evans points out, Thersites accompanies all major scenes of the play on the barest of excuses and as an "adviser of our awareness" is "the strongest force of unity in the play; perhaps the sole unifying force."[2] Thus the prime satirist's influence strongly pervades act I even when he is not physically present. Ulysses goes on to dissect the satiric attack on the Greek establishment: "They tax our policy and call it cowardice . . ." He accuses the satirists (with Thersites as their unstated leader) of opposing the well-drawn plans of generals like himself and making a mockery of the principles of reason. Satire, as Ulysses sees it and as it works throughout the play, upsets the Right Reason of the Renaissance and jars the smooth hierarchies of the Elizabethan World Picture by shaking that "degree" which provides the respectful binding for the traditional ladder of high design. Satirists are irreverently free thinkers. They represent inward rebellion based on an individual, independent conception of morality.[3]

THE CURSE OF REALISM

Of all the characters in Shakespeare whom I have called satirists, Thersites least requires proof of fulfilling that role. As Miss Randolph says,

[2] Bertrand Evans, *Shakespeare's Comedies* (1960), pp. 184–185.

[3] Paul N. Siegal, *Shakespearean Tragedy and the Elizabethan Compromise* (1957), p. 62, discusses both the troublesome Puritans and the Italianates (Catholic free thinkers) of the period as malcontent challengers of Humanism who sometimes functioned as lawless satirists; their "unbridled individualism was destructive to the ideal of an integrated hierarchical society."

More than any other malcontent, railer, or satirist of the time,
Thersites reverts to the primitive satiric principle, marring
and harming the human body. Bricriu of the Poison Tongue
might very well have spoken these lines for him: "If thou
use to beat me, I will begin at thy heel and tell what thou art
by inches, thou thing of no bowels, thou" (II, i, 52–54).
Thersites' more formal curses, those having the dignity of an
invocation and an "Amen," call down in primitive fashion
the most repulsive of diseases.[4]

Thersites exhibits an unusual determination, even for
the most bitter of our satirists. He will not settle for the
ineffectual laughter-purging role of the fool, even if other
characters refer to him as such.[5] He voices this in a strategic appearance *solus* before Achilles' tent, II, iii.

> How now, Thersites? What, lost in the labyrinth of
> thy fury? Shall the elephant Ajax carry it thus? He
> beats me, and I rail at him. O worthy satisfaction!
> Would it were otherwise: that I could beat him
> whilst he rail'd at me. 'Sfoot, I'll learn to conjure
> and raise devils but I'll see some issue of my special
> execrations.

So motivated is he to make an impression on his society
that he determines to resort to the dangerous forces of
magic to give his railing real satiric power. He is as de-

[4] Mary Claire Randolph, "The Medical Concept in English
Renaissance Satiric Theory" (1941), pp. 152–153.

[5] Robert Hillis Goldsmith, *Wise Fools* (1963), p. 71, says this
railing-buffoon satirist is called a fool because "Shakespeare must
translate an earlier, traditional role into terms familiar to his Elizabethan audiences. Thersites wears no bells or bauble, nor does he
sprinkle his wit with nonsense in the customary manner of the
court or stage fool."

termined a satirist as old Margaret (of *Richard III*) was a determined curser. The difference here lies in the now complete submergence of magic in the sea of psychological realism to which we now turn.

In Thersites' world all evil cannot conveniently abide in one diabolical cause of unrest, one usurper, one villain. His moral order yields up far greater causal complexities. Moreover, it is not a narrow personal vengeance that fires Thersites' curses, but a wide-ranging perception of the true moral identity of his fellows. In every case, he has merely to verbalize character sketches of individuals, i.e., to *say who they are*, and these people proceed to give effect to the curses on them simply by *being themselves*.[6] Thus the satirist who is so ready to resort to magic for power ironically has least need to do so.

Many of the realistic curses that strengthen the satire within the play first appear in act II and are worked out later as each character brings his own curse down on himself. In the very opening scene of act II Thersites had called down the conventional satiric blights of bile, plague and itch on Agamemnon, Ajax and Achilles (ll.1–25). In the context of a raillery competition with Ajax, none of this has much specific import, although a metaphoric disease does indeed spread among the Greeks. But when alone, as in his pledge (scene iii) to see the "issue" of his

[6] James G. Rice, "Shakespeare's Curse" (1947), p. 234, sees in this play a marked change in Shakespeare's curse pattern: "Whereas the predominant pattern of the curses in the earlier plays is 'May evil come to you as to me,' there is a growing emphasis in the later plays on the idea that the transgression will finally work its own punishment" as in II, iii, 3–21, and later in *Timon of Athens*.

execrations, Thersites aims his uniquely well-pointed barbs. He begins with Achilles:

> Then there's Achilles, a rare enginer. If Troy be not taken till these two [Achilles and Ajax] undermine it, the walls will stand till they fall of themselves. O thou great thunder-darter of Olympus, forget that thou art Jove, the king of gods, and, Mercury, lose all the serpentine craft of thy caduceus, if ye take not that little little less than little wit from them that they have! which short-arm'd ignorance itself knows is so abundant scarce it will not in circumvention deliver a fly from a spider without drawing their massy irons and cutting the web.
>
> (II, iii, 8–19)

Unlike Ulysses' emptily eloquent rationalistic attack on Achilles, Thersites' invective is emotionally charged with the satirically sharp and accurate character sketch. Earlier (II, i) he had, with less vehemence, struck at Achilles for his weak wit and overreliance on brawn. We have only to anticipate Achilles' brutal murder and mutilation of Hector to see how he ignobly lives up to this evaluation, this curse of realism.

Patroclus makes the theme of the realistic curse even more obvious when he enters (scene iii) ready to rail with Thersites—evidently for sport and as a simple purgative for his own resentments. Thersites, always the coward, assumes the tone of heedless raillery, but begins,

> Thyself upon thyself! The common curse of mankind, folly and ignorance, be thine in great revenue!

> Heaven bless thee from a tutor, and discipline come
> not near thee! Let thy blood be thy direction till
> thy death! Then if she that lays thee out says thou
> art a fair corse, I'll be sworn and sworn upon't she
> never shrouded any but lazars. Amen.
>
> (29–38)

Patroclus mocks his "amen," but Thersites has been quite
serious in employing the strong curse framework of the
prayer structure. In the rest of the play Patroclus does
indeed follow the sanguinary lead of his own character—
from Achilles' bed out onto the battlefield to meet the
death Thersites ordained.

Although Thersites continues to be our "glass" for ob-
serving and interpreting individual characters and actions,[7] he makes a general curse in this key scene which
sets out the design for the fabric of the whole play:

> After this, the vengeance on the whole camp! or
> rather the Neapolitan bone-ache! for that methinks
> is the curse dependent on those who war for a plack-
> et. . . . All the argument is a whore and a cuckold—
> a good quarrel to draw emulous factions and bleed
> to death upon. Now, the dry suppeago on the sub-
> ject, and war and lechery confound all!
>
> (20–22, 78–82)

With these words echoing from the tradition of the
powerful old Celtic satirists (who so often cursed their
victims with diseases) the rest of the Greeks enter. With
them comes Calchas—whose appearance in the plot sets

[7] Eustace M. W. Tillyard, *Shakespeare's Problem Plays* (1961),
p. 61, among others, disagrees, relegating Thersites to the role of a
relatively inconsequential, bitter, fool.

the death mark on the love of Troilus and Cressida and
initiates the confused, unsatisfactory conclusion to the
war's stalemate. The characters plot their own desperate
war tale and bitter love story; yet it is somehow Thersites' curse that spreads the germs inherent in their diseased world.

INFECTION

Hope in both the love and war plots runs highest during
act IV in which Thersites does not appear. Though Agamemnon made light of the "slave," and though Ajax
seems to regard him as a bearer of good luck who should
be retained, Thersites functions in the play as a bearer
only of the satiric curse whose ruling metaphor is disease. Acting the part of the fool for others, he only appears to fulfill the possible comic expectations of his role;
in reality—the reality revealed in soliloquy and by the
play's structure and conclusion—this true satirist makes
himself felt through hurt if not through tragedy.

At the end of act IV the lovers, though parted, have
vowed fidelity, and hope remains that they will be reunited. Moreover, scene v leaves the supposed warring
Greek and Trojan generals carrousing with the greatest
of friendliness in the Greek camp after the revealed kinship of Ajax and Hector stops their combat. With Thersites' gloomy words totally absent from this section we
recognize something like the traditional act IV of tragedy
where one's hopes of a happy conclusion are conventionally raised before the final crash of the last act.

But the last part of *Troilus and Cressida* does not afford
even the pitiful or terrible satisfaction of the tragic dis-

aster. Not death, but corroding, degrading disease comes with this kind of crash. Not surprisingly, Thersites is everywhere, on the barest of excuses, chorically infecting more and more of the people whose character has already doomed them to the bitterest conclusion.

As usual, for the keynote we turn to the satirist's prose soliloquy. Wittily sparring with Achilles and Patroclus at the start of the first scene of act V, Thersites (as earlier) appears harmless enough. But left alone, he turns upon his two keepers, as he had turned on Ajax, angles in on their faults, and reasserts his intentions to harm them with his own unique weapons:

> With too much blood and too little brain these two may run mad; but if with too much brain and too little blood they do, I'll be a curer of madmen.[8]

Thersites is *not* a curer of the madness in the play. In clinching the pronouncement on the sanguinary fury of Patroclus and Achilles, he disavows the role of physician sometimes attributed to or claimed by the more sophisticated satirists (e.g., in the verse apologiae of Horace, Juvenal, Persius). In fact, as one critic observes, the entire world of *Troilus and Cressida* "has fallen the whole way down, past hope, past cure, and physicianless."[9] Thersites adheres to the more primitive function of the dis-

[8] Lines 53–56; Oscar James Campbell, *Shakespeare's Satire* (1963), p. 107, otherwise condemning Thersites as a clown whose judgments usually mean little, selects this passage as an exception; here Thersites "is presenting Shakespeare's thesis and providing the audience with a standard by which to judge the conduct of the pair and to understand its utter vanity."

[9] Evans, p. 167.

easer.[10] In this case, it is only Shakespeare, as we shall see, who can be called the curative Satirist-physician.

Still alone, but looking toward the approaching group, Thersites yet has the freedom to condemn Agamemnon and Menelaus too. One's wisdom and the other's dignity prove absurd illusions:

> Here's Agamemnon, an honest fellow enough and one that loves quails, but he has not so much brain as earwax; and the goodly transformation of Jupiter there, his brother, the bull, the primitive statue and oblique memorial of cuckolds, a thrifty shoeing horn in a chain, hanging at his brother's leg—to what form but that he is should wit larded with malice, and malice forced with wit, turn him to? To an ass were nothing; he is both ass and ox: to an ox were nothing; he is both ox and ass. To be a dog, a mule, a cat, a fitchook, a toad, a lizard, an owl, a puttock, or a herring without a roe, I would not care; but to be Menelaus, I would conspire against destiny. Ask me not what I would be if I were not Thersites; for I care not to be the louse of a lazar, so I were not Menelaus.
>
> (V, i, 53–72)

The device of the invidious comparison of course harkens back to the primitive curser's reputed ability to make the stated transformations of his victims into various loathesome animals. Thersites suggests that he would like to

[10] Rice, p. 180, traces Thersites' favorite curses back to the medieval type of "vengeance-disease" curse from which the "pox curse" developed (to call down venereal disease as God's punishment for sexual excess or depravity).

turn all objects of his contempt into such cowardly cuck-
olds as Menelaus and then, in the *solus* speech that caps
the scene, widens his attack to include some Trojans—
Diomedes and Cressida:

> That same Diomed's a false-hearted rogue, a most
> unjust knave. I will no more trust him when he leers
> than I will a serpent when he hisses. He will spend
> his mouth and promise, like Brabbler the hound; but
> when he performs, astronomers foretell it; it is
> prodigious, there will come some change. The sun
> borrows of the moon when Diomed keeps his word.
> I will rather leave to see Hector than not to dog him.
> They say he keeps a Troyan drab and uses the traitor
> Calchas' tent. I'll after. Nothing but lechery! All
> incontinent varlots!
>
> (96–107)

As Thersites' attacks spread like disease to strike more
representatives of his society, they begin to take on the
moralistic phrasing traditional to such satiric invective
even while their language continues to be harsh.

If, during the fourth act, we hoped to escape the influence of the satirist, the final act only brings on Thersites' plaguing voice with a continuing, accelerating in-
sistence. As a tragic Fate looms, unavoidable, at the end
of the tragedy, so the controlling satirist reigns at the
end of the satire-drama. The difference lies in the drama-
turgy, for while tragedy classically works up to the dis-
aster that brings fast death, satire only works up to a
degree of morbidity in disease; we infer that the prog-
nosis is bad, but we are denied the assurance and, yes,
the satisfaction, of beholding the finality of death.

Since only rarely does a playwright attempt such a precarious structure as the satire-drama which does not seesaw into tragedy or comedy, it will be worthwhile to continue tracing our diligent satirist's progress through the play's crisis, climax and denouement—tainted as they are with the peculiar stain of satire. Scene ii, the witnessed infidelity of Cressida, I pinpoint as the play's crisis. Scene iv, Thersites on the battlefield, the climax—such as it is; scene vi, the long awaited encounter of Hector and Achilles, comes as an anticlimax, and Hector's murder in viii an ironic denouement. Such must be the odd structure adopted by the authorial satirist seeking to avoid the conventional grooves of tragedy.

The scene (ii) in which Troilus and Ulysses spy on Cressida's tryst with Diomedes and are in turn overseen by Thersites is undoubtedly the play's dramatic highlight. Its tone as satiric crisis depends on (1) the quality of Troilus's reactions to the love scene he watches, and (2) the nature of the overall comments added by the satirist who dogs them all. Beginning with the latter, we note that Thersites' off-color yet moralistic exclamations punctuate the entire scene with marks of condemnation. His first comment makes a sexual metaphor out of the musical one Ulysses used to excuse Cressida's upsetting overfamiliarity with Diomedes. Thersites: "And any man may *sing* her, if he can take her *cliff*. She's *noted*" (line 11). He achieves a downgrading effect by running the musical (sing) through the suggestive (cliff, or key) into a final submersion in the unavoidably insulting (noted, or mark of infamy). By insisting on this type of sexual word-play he continues to interpret and expose a possible love scene as just another ugly bit of lechery. When

Cressida, perhaps sweetly, asks her keeper, "What would you have me do?", Thersites leeringly comments, "A juggling trick—to be secretly open" (line 24). Shorter exclamations are more succinct in conveying the overviewer's judgment and curse: "Roguery!" (line 19, of Cressida); "O plague and madness!" (line 35, of Cressida's whispering). Or he may combine the sexually metaphoric slur with the succinct moralistic curse, as when, after Troilus insists on staying on to watch more of the seduction, the satirist seems to condemn both whore and voyeur:

> How the devil luxury, with his fat rump
> and potato finger, tickles these together!
> Fry, lechery, fry!
>
> (55–57)

And before Cressida exits she acknowledges that the self-curse by which she swore (III, ii) and reswore (IV, ii) her fidelity will now come down on her in the form of moral disease: "I shall be plagu'd"—which also suggests the leper-Cressid of Henryson's popular poem.

At this point, Troilus remains as the chief bearer of traditional principles and moral ideals; for the rest of the scene Thersites ruthlessly punches holes in Troilus's precious chivalry.[11] The "credence" and "esperance" in his heart are the ideals which conflict with and "invert th'attest of eyes and ears." Cressida's blatant infidelity topples that idolatry of womanhood (line 129) which medieval chivalry bequeathed to the Renaissance. When Troilus suggests that this might not have been Cressida

[11] In scene iii, Troilus is so identified with chivalric ideals that he makes his entrance on Hector's pronouncing the important word "honour" (l.28).

at all, Thersites flails this vestigial idealism with the flatly empirical seventeenth-century question: "Will 'a swagger himself out on's own eyes?" (line 136)—reminding us of satirist Falstaff's similar opposition to abstract concepts and ideals and his reliance on sensuous evidence.[12] Already undercut, Troilus launches into his high-toned speech denying all he has just seen and heard in the names of beauty, soul, sanctimonious vows, the gods, and unity itself. Ulysses makes a sympathetic audience for this discourse on the revolt of reason against authority, since it deals with the theme of his earlier speech on Degree. Troilus's passionate involvement in the problem Ulysses had so intellectually stated causes a schizophrenic division in him which typifies the "sickness" of the fading Renaissance days.

Troilus builds his rhetoric into the heroic frenzy that prompts him to take the traditional vengeance of sword on Diomedes for stealing his "divine" lady. Thersites has only to add the final punctuation, "He'll tickle it [the sword] for his concupy," and the inflated world of chivalry cracks under the undeniable weight of this realistic, one-line version of the courtly love story. Immediately, Troilus breaks into a bewailing of the "false, false, false" Cressida when Thersites thus exposes the fragility of the old ideals. As the play's acute love satire blends into its war satire Thersites is allowed to summarize: "Lechery, lechery! still wars and lechery! Nothing else holds fashion. A burning devil take them!" The object of his final

---

[12] S. L. Bethell, *Shakespeare and the Popular Dramatic Tradition* (1948), p. 101, calls Thersites "a scurrilous chorus upon the futility of war—a role comparable to that of Falstaff in the battle scenes of *Henry IV, Part 1*."

curse has spread to an indefinitely inclusive plural pronoun. Such a speech, as Bethell says, surely is a way "to commend the opinion of Thersites to our very serious attention."[13] In this play Shakespeare was dealing the same death blows—perhaps even more bitterly—to chivalric philosophy as was his contemporary, Cervantes. The tone is definitely that of the Counter-Renaissance.

When battle finally begins, in scene iv, Thersites provides the preface as well as the antiheroic action. Alone on stage he begins the scene with a two-part speech, railing first at three Trojans with their ragged love missions, then at four Greeks with their wrangling politics. He debunks Troilus with the mocking synecdoche that equates the knight to his sleeve—the symbol of his torn chivalric love. Thersites debunks the other knights, warriors and ladies by calling them asses, dogs, whores, whoremasters. When Troilus and Diomedes actually cross swords over possession of the lady Cressida, Thersites cheers them both down from their knightly eminences with "Hold thy whore, Grecian! Now for thy whore, Troyan!" And after the mighty Hector has broken the opposition of wife, father and sister with high talk about defending his honor, on the battlefield who does he challenge first? Thersites. The satirist, of course, quickly denies being "of blood and honour," i.e., a match for Hector, and saves his neck by realistically giving his true character: "No, no! I am a rascal, a scurvy railing knave, a very filthy rogue." Then he off-handedly puts a curse on Hector's life.

In the rest of the battle scenes the realistic curses all come home and Thersites' view of society prevails. Many

13 Bethell, p. 101.

Greeks fall. Patroclus dies. And Hector is finally slaugh-
tered ignominiously by Achilles' henchmen after the absurdly anticlimactic, long-awaited first armed encounter
between the two titans (scene vi) when Achilles seems to
fumble his sword and Hector is obviously weary. All we
have of the battle between the original foes in love,
Menelaus and Paris, is Thersites' appraisal:

> The cuckold and the cuckold-maker are at it.
> Now, bull! now, dog! 'Loo, Paris, 'loo!
> Now my double henn'd sparrow! 'Loo, Paris,
> 'loo! The bull has the game, Ware horns, ho!
>
> (V, vii, 9–13)

And all the bloodshed does not end the war nor the
enmity among men. Hector's death does not give the
Greeks a decisive victory because the spoils were the
abstract ones of the honor code, not the tangible city
of Troy or the person of Helen. And all honor has shown
itself infected with human fallibility and moral baseness.
A bitter, disillusioned Troilus in the last scene dully asks
the gods for brief plagues and marches home still bearing
an unpurged hatred for Diomedes and carrying Troy's
unrelieved hope of revenge on Greece. He furiously casts
the pandar's curse at Pandarus (who had set it up for
himself earlier), and the festering Pandarus pronounces
the play's last word—"diseases," which is the mark of
Thersites.

CONTAGION, NOT CATHARSIS

What is the meaning of the strange, bitter, unclassifiable
ending? Jan Kott tells us what it conspicuously lacks:

In tragedy the protagonists die, but the moral order is preserved. Their death confirms the existence of the absolute. In this amazing play Troilus neither dies himself, nor does he kill the unfaithful Cressida. There is no catharsis. Even the death of Hector is not fully tragic—but ironic.[14]

Other critics, such as Paul Kendall, agree that the chief feature of this play is its "grim, ironic, rueful and sometimes mordant commentary upon life." He goes on to note that it somehow reaches out from the stage in an unusual manner: "In departing from the clear pattern of comedy and tragedy and approaching the blurred design of life itself, Shakespeare evokes the participation of the audience."[15]

But what is the nature of this "participation"? Surely all audiences react to all plays and thereby participate even while they do not move, speak, or perhaps even weep or laugh. What makes *Troilus and Cressida* different? In working thus with aesthetic affect, George Taylor as a reader asks, I think, the right question: "Why does one put the play down with revulsion of feeling towards it stronger than towards any other Elizabethan treatment of the same theme?"[16] He goes on to suggest that, more than any other, this play "reduces love and honour to laughter and scorn." While such an answer falls in with the general argument here, it does not go deeply enough into the mechanics of audience response and the aesthetic

[14] Jan Kott, *Shakespeare Our Contemporary* (1964), p. 74.

[15] Paul M. Kendall, "Inaction and Ambivalence in *Troilus and Cressida*," *English Studies in Honor of James Southall Wilson* (1951), p. 144. William Witherle Lawrence, "Troilus, Cressida and Thersites" (1942), p. 435, agrees that Thersites speaks truths and that (p. 433) Shakespeare meant his gibes to affect the audience.

[16] George C. Taylor, "Shakespeare's Attitude Towards Love and Honor in *Troilus and Cressida*" (1930), p. 783.

significance of the unique kind of participation under examination.

In the last section we traced the spreading infection of Thersites' influence—his cynical world view. There is some doubt about the authenticity of the play's last speech (and final scenes),[17] but I would agree with Robert Ornstein who studies the play as a Jacobean document and thinks its ending shapes a dialectical drama:

The comic complaints of a syphilitic bawd end the play on a note of derision that seems to vindicate Thersites' scabrous cynicism. Yet the total impression of *Troilus* is hardly nihilistic. It is a depressing play, not because it establishes the futility of man's search for ideal values but because it is a sociological and psychological analysis of decadent values.[18]

But this drama differs from the other problem plays (*All's Well* and *Measure for Measure*) because it lacks the redemptive elements of romantic comedy and the conclusion in which "vice is unmasked, social abuses are corrected, the audience is left edified and ethically satisfied."[19] Instead, Thersites forces on the audience what has been called "a painful division of mind"[20] because, coarse and revolting as he is, he bares truths.

Tillyard blames the play's unsatisfying quality on Shakespeare's over-reliance on his sources (Chaucer and Lydgate) which give too much weight to Troilus' part.[21] But why assume that such a consummate craftsman,

[17] William Witherle Lawrence, *Shakespeare's Problem Comedies*, (1960), p. 125.

[18] Robert Ornstein, *The Moral Vision of Jacobean Tragedy* (1965), p. 249.

[19] Siegel, p. 211.

[20] Kendall, p. 140.

[21] Tillyard, *Shakespeare's Problem Plays*, p. 63.

working with such a familiar story, after the success of *Hamlet*, would make such an elementary error? It is more fruitful to assume that Shakespeare, as usual, was trying something new and worked precisely for the odd effect he achieved. Kendall argues that Shakespeare was not at the mercy of his source materials, but deliberately adopted *inaction* as an ordering principle of the play.[22] There is no vent in action, either tragic or comic, for any of the hatreds aroused: the Ajax-Hector combat is broken off; a suffering Troilus is frustrated in his attempt to relieve his hatred of Diomedes; Hector's death is a miserable, inglorious act; and everywhere Thersites undermines the honor and worth of the acts of men and women. Campbell describes one aspect of this lack of cathartic action and conjectures its purpose:

The purgation and reform of Achilles hoped for by Ulysses and expected in a comic-satiric ending does not take place. Only the tempest of grief and rage aroused by the murder of Patroclus drives him back to battle. Then he acts not like a soldier but like a man wild with anger. So, Ulysses' nicely devised plan to force Achilles to resume his social duties fails. The outcome, as in the case of all the plans of the other characters, whether wise or foolish, is futility, and was meant to awaken the scornful laughter of satire.[23]

But the scornful laughter with which Jonson and Marston were then reforming and purging their plays' moral delinquents simply does not come off in the same way here. O. J. Campbell perceived the relationship between the 1599 Bishop's Restraining Order on satire and the flourishing of satire in the drama, but he then insists on

[22] Kendall, p. 133.
[23] O. J. Campbell, *Shakespeare's Satire*, pp. 104–105.

squeezing Shakespeare's play into the conventional mold:
as the scornful laughter of author and audience ejected
evil men and women at the play's end, so, Campbell says,
are Troilus and Cressida dismissed: the "conventions of
dramatic satire" hold true; it is just that in this play
"Shakespeare divested the convention of all its obvious
features."[24] No. Rather than denuding a convention, it
is obvious that Shakespeare was using that convention
in a new way.

Hegel traces the drama, or social play, to the ancient
satyric drama with its mixed tragic-comic roots. He explains that when combined, rather than merely juxta-
posed, to form the social play, the two contradictory
points of view mutually accommodate and blunt the force
of their opposition. And in such a truly dialectical drama
there is the "danger of breaking away from the true dramatic type, or ceasing to be genuine poetry."[25] *Troilus
and Cressida* leaped far ahead of its time in risking dramatic form, propriety and success for the sake of its intellectual, socially critical content.

In it, Shakespeare denies us the tragic hero, the bloody
purge of evil, the scornfully comic laugh fest, and even
the satisfaction of emotionally kicking a scapegoat until
our aroused passions are lulled. Instead, he lets the satirist (magically) infect more and more of the characters,
who (realistically) already carried the germs of their own
destruction, only far enough to parade an entirely "sick"
play world. The audience can then reject this world—as
many have—on some fabricated basis of aesthetic un-

[24] O. J. Campbell, *Shakespeare's Satire*, p. 118.
[25] Friedrich Hegel, *On Tragedy*, Anne and Henry Paolucci, eds.
(1962), pp. 57–58.

orthodoxy, or it can "take" the disease. If the satire becomes contagious, as it should, the audience and readers will see themselves in the play's mirror, see in it their own corrupt society, and be moved to the *action* which has been frustrated in the play. All of the aroused hatred and censure of all of its suffering characters will spring out of the theater into the streets.

6: The Satirist's Purgation in
Timon of Athens

SHAKESPEARE'S *Life of Timon of Athens* is cast in the form of a tragedy depicting the fall and subsequent death of a great man. If we grant Aristotle's theory of tragedy general credibility, it must apply to this play as well as to *Oedipus Rex*, *Othello* or *Lear*. But the hero's erratic behavior modifies our admiration of him. At his death we feel a certain release of pity for the complete ruination of a once noble gentleman but nothing of the Aristotelian terror. Satire laces the tragedy everywhere and it is not surprising that the particular nature of the hero, which becomes that of the satirist, qualifies the drama as tragedy.

From the very beginning satiric undertones differentiate the tone from the conventionally taut, dreadful, celebratory tragic voice. In the keynote first scene minor characters extol the virtues of their patron, the hero, but the obvious satiric undertone of the compliments made by Poet, Painter, Jeweller and Merchant undercuts the tragic construction and warns us of this play's peculiar emphasis. The Poet composes for fat fees what must be empty praising verses though he callously admits that in so doing he devalues poetry. The Painter's portrait (perhaps of Timon) "is a pretty mockery of life" (l. 35), not just a good representation of its subject.[1] The play's primary satirist, philosophic cynic Apemantus, comes railing onstage in this same scene. Moreover, we find minor characters named Lucilius and Varro—surely references to the founders of the satiric tradition in which Shakespeare is working here. And III, ii includes an explicit comment on the degradation of the times which implies an allusion to the lost Golden Age theme so commonly noted in satire. There are even satiric attacks on what I shall identify as specific activities of the court of James I.

All of these interlacing satiric elements appear well before we witness the phenomenon of the tragic hero as satirist, which does not come until III, vi when the rudely disillusioned Timon feasts his so-called friends on water. Before tracing the development to this conversion scene, however, let us get an overview on the problem at hand.

The tendency of the tragedy to arouse pity and terror is mitigated by the fact that in the course of the play the hero becomes a raging satirist. One particular aspect of his character as satirist brings about his demise, and that is of course his extreme misanthropy. But it is his whole identity as a satirist which operates as his tragic *haemartia*.

We are not so interested in the play's tragic structure per se, stressing the Aristotelian purging of pity and terror (which is not very remarkable here anyway), but in its analogue—the satiric catharsis of hatred and cen-

[1] And see H. J. Oliver, ed., *The Arden Shakespeare: Timon of Athens* (1959), p. 14, for a gloss on "mocked."

sure postulated in Chapter I. As it happens, however, these are released almost in tandem with the tragic emotions and constantly parallel the tragic structure. Early satiric elements tend toward subtlety, but in the last two acts as Timon nears his inevitable death, the satire gains in virulence and power. The satirist-hero's death, as we shall see, is necessary to complete the purgation of hatred and censure aroused in the play.

The play neatly divides into two parts which outline for us the making of the satirist: the first half, in Athens, represents the illusionary or ideal phase of the satirist's "life" (I–II with III as transition) while the second half (IV–V), outside of Athens, shows the disillusioned satirist entangled in his new and bitter view of reality. It has been said that Timon's tragedy "is not that he is reduced to poverty and cast off, but that the godlike image of man in his heart is cast down, and his dreams of human fellowship destroyed."[2] A kind of formula underlies the play's essential structure: *Illusion plus disillusion, in the presence of the catalytic satirist* (Apemantus) *yields the tragic satirist.*

Thus the much criticized artifice involved in the depiction of Timon's exaggerated munificence at the play's beginning is explained as the schematization of the golden age of a satirist's development. In order to convey the sense of the ideal so strong in Timon, Shakespeare must exaggerate even at the sacrifice of realism. Timon's world view, including his ideas about the nobility of his fellow man, is the old golden ideal every satirist has within him or the utopian vision which he at some time conceives.

[2] Peter Alexander, *Shakespeare's Life and Art* (London, 1939), p. 184, quoted by H. J. Oliver, p. xlvii.

In this phase all men are virtuous and matters of finance exist in a fairyland of medieval affluence. A Godlike nobility flows downward from the true aristocrat, permeating all lower levels with the gentle virtues of morality, reason and faith. The ideal Renaissance gentleman, nobleman or governor, a true Lorenzo to his adoring artists, could expect from life only beauty, harmony and fidelity. This is the Timon we meet.

The rude discovery of "true" human nature comes in a parablelike manner with the loss of Timon's gold. The incredibility of his lack of foresight in the matter, like his blind faith in his flattering friends, is a necessary part of the stylized contrast Shakespeare makes to compose his satirist-hero. But it is natural that the impact of reality should be shown with a certain amount of realism, including significant barbed references to contemporary conditions.

Among these realistic details the revelation of the havoc created by modern usury looms large. According to J. W. Draper,[3] *Timon* graphically dramatizes the effect of the new middle-class money-lenders on the socio-economic fabric of Elizabethan society. The old order broke up as its inherited large parcels of land were enclosed; the new interest rates of the upstart merchant class drained its wealth. Timon is the typical nobleman whose wealth lies in his lands, who is a good soldier, comes of a great house, and refers to his reign as that of a prince. The usurers who ruin him are typically "knaves," "slaves," "peasants." Draper calls the play "Shakespeare's *Gulliver*" and explains it as "a sort of dramatic elegy on the ideals

[3] John W. Draper "The Theme of *Timon of Athens*" (1934), pp. 28–30 *passim*.

of chivalry that were succumbing in a capitalistic age."
In this view, the senate's appeal to Timon to return from
his self-imposed banishment is symbolic of their need for
the return of the ancient chivalric virtues—honor and
valor. But the age of retribution has come.

With its ostensible subject ancient Athens, the play
really directs itself, by what must have been fairly obvious references, to Shakespeare's contemporary society
—specifically alluding to the court of James I. At Timon's
entertainments (I, ii), for example, "Cupid" introduces a
"masque of Ladies as Amazons, with lutes in their hands,
dancing and playing." The Arden editor merely notes
that the masque was a popular form of court entertain-
ment and that its appearance in ancient Athens is a
typical Shakespearean anachronism. As with the striking
clock in *Julius Caesar*,[4] there must be more here than
Shakespeare's whimsical admixture of cultures (or his
ignorance of social history). The masque presented to
flatter[5] Timon appears to be as irrelevant, frivolous and
lacking in dramatic content as most of those paraded at
James's court. Indeed, upon the masquers' appearance,
instead of the celebratory music conventionally used to
highlight this moment in the performance,[6] we have
Apemantus's satiric comment:

[4] Sigurd Burckhardt, *Shakespearean Meanings* (1968), pp. 3–21,
shows how the play's clock strikes upon the "old style" in a time
that is profoundly "out of joint."

[5] Timon speaks of being entertained with his "own device"
which may mean he conceived the idea for this masque just as
the Stuarts often did for theirs; see, e.g., Jonson's *Masque of
Queens* or *Oberon*.

[6] Jonson often had his masquers "discovered" under great shells,
inside animals and other massy trick props designed by Inigo
Jones.

What a sweep of vanity comes this way!
They dance? They are mad women.
Like madness is the glory of this life,
As this pomp shows to a little oil and root.
We make ourselves fools to disport ourselves,
And spend our flatteries to drink those men
Upon whose age we void it up again
With poisonous spite and envy.
Who lives that's not depraved or depraves?
Who dies that bears not one spurn to their graves
Of their friend's gift?

(I, ii, 137–147)

The stage direction that follows becomes ironic: "The Lords rise from table, with much adoring of Timon; and to show their loves, each single out an Amazon, and all dance, men with women, a lofty strain or two to the hautboys, and cease." Shakespeare's indirect targets of attack may include Ben Jonson and Inigo Jones as well as the sponsoring king himself, but in the larger picture, the opulent figureheads for an entire degenerating society are hereby exposed.[7] The satirist's final lines on the masque prophetically pierce the curtain of the future for seventeenth-century English royalty, as well as for Timon:

I should fear those that dance before me now
Would one day stamp upon me. 'T has been done.
Men shut their doors against a setting sun.

(148–150)

---

[7] The early Stuarts, ostentatious patrons of the arts, drained England's treasury with the vast expenses of these masques; Flavius explicitly criticizes this kind of heedless extravagance in I, ii, 197 ff.

All of the plays examined in this study have included various kinds of satiric "teams" with an established satirist influencing or converting another character to the satiric persuasion. These relationships have been intense (Margaret-Elizabeth), casual (Jaques-Touchstone-Orlando), ambiguous (Falstaff-Hal), clear-cut (Thersites-many characters), but they have always been willful. In *Timon*, however, the elements of extreme Illusion and abrupt Disillusionment need only the catalytic presence of a confirmed satirist to bring about the conversion. The tragic satirist Timon is the product of this dramatic chemistry; he undergoes rapid and total character change while the catalytic satirist Apemantus remains constant.

Apemantus's appearances in act I quickly establish the high and solid quality of his satiric interests. Immediately in the scene with Poet and Painter he "keeps us from being dazzled by the deceptive splendor which might cause us to mistake pretentious parade for noble generosity."[8] He identifies himself as a Philosopher and Cynic and in the manner traditional to strong satirists he curses his city, especially its merchants (line 245), women (puns at lines 205 and 210), and leaders. When Alcibiades enters, Apemantus curses and immediately draws out the philosophic generalization:

> *So, so, there!*
> *Aches contract and starve your supple joints!*
> *That there should be small love amongst these sweet*
> *   knaves,*
> *And all this courtesy! The strain of man's bred out*
> *Into baboon and monkey.*

(I, i, 256–260)

[8] Oscar James Campbell, *Shakespeare's Satire*, p. 188.

His chief emotions are hatred (line 236) and anger (line 241) which he vents by his vehement censure of modern mankind. His railing "arouses and directs the derision of the spectators"[9] and has the moral slant expected of the legitimate satirist. We note, for example, that Apemantus will accept nothing from Timon's coffers, as he says, "for if I should be brib'd too, there would be none left to rail upon thee, and then thou wouldst sin the faster" (I, ii, 244–246). Moreover, with the honest steward Flavius, he functions in the tradition of the good advisor to the prince, much like Euvular ("good counselor") from *Gorboduc* who was contrasted with the flatterer Philander.

After act I Apemantus only has two more important scenes, the first of which has puzzled critics because of its intrusive nature. The cynic turns up in II, ii in a dialogue with an otherwise unmentioned Fool which takes place while offstage Flavius gives Timon the sad account of his financial status. The Fool-Apemantus exchanges are very much like the scenes between Touchstone and Jaques. But the glitter and enthusiasm are missing. Unlike the melancholy Jaques, Apemantus does not envy the Fool's license and clearly considers himself superior, though he feels a certain kinship of wits. The Fool's cleverest remark doesn't come up to Touchstone's weakest; and, instead of excitement, it only elicits the satirist's egoistic compliment, "That answer might have become Apemantus" (II, ii, 126). The targets of their witticisms are mostly the usurers who are under attack throughout the play. But Timon himself comes in for some debunking through identification with the scene's

[9] Ibid., p. 187.

ruling metaphor: the Fool.[10] The insult in being called a
Fool involves the subject's wisdom and independence.
Timon soon admits to having been "unwise" though not
ignoble in his generosity (line 183), and it is evident
throughout the play's first half that he is ignobly tied
to his "friends" with the manacles of usurious interest
rates and insincerity. Apemantus, on the other hand,
wisely sees through facades and independently disassoci-
ates himself from the social status of the fool with its
obligations to "lover, elder brother and woman" (II, ii,
130). He remains stable and independent, and therefore
morally healthy, even in his preoccupation with folly and
degeneracy.

He makes his other major appearance in his long
dialogue with the self-banished Timon, just after Alcibiades' visit and before that of the faithful Flavius (IV,
iii). Unlike other satiric teams we have examined, here
the first satirist tries to dissuade the second from the
calling rather than to teach and recommend him to it.
He seems positively annoyed that Timon affects and uses
his "manners" (line 199) and considers Timon's misanthropy the mere result of a suddenly unbalanced melancholy humor (line 203)—i.e., a psychological sickness
and not the genuine article. Yet one suspects that Apemantus is secretly pleased to have influenced by example
so great a man; the dialogue, in fact, can be read so that

---

[10] The Fool asks if he will be left at Timon's (line 95). Apemantus replies, "If Timon stay at home," which H. J. Oliver glosses:
"*Either* so long as Timon is at home there will be a fool there *or*
I shall leave you there if Timon be there to provide fitting company
for you" (p. 43). Timon's servant is called a "fool and fit for thy
master" when he berates Lucullus for refusing Timon a loan (III,
i, 52).

Apemantus is really testing the authenticity of Timon's pose. How else can we explain Apemantus' sincere reply, "I love thee better now than e're I did," to the insistent anger and insults the new misanthrope projects? A touch of Falstaff's pride in Hal endures in this relationship, and Timon remains even more unrelenting than the young prince.

Something important seems to be at stake in their extended contest in scurrility.[11] For a long while the "rogue hereditary" (274) and the nouveau satirist[12] show themselves equally matched in the linguistic skills of curse and invective. Since Timon is a man of extremes (see line 300), his more dogged hatred (accompanied by stones) eventually drives his visitor away. But Apemantus wins the contest in another manner when he announces he will tell Athens that Timon has gold again, thereby luring people to vex the man-hater and try his misanthropy to the limit (line 394). The ensuing encounters with the banditti and with Flavius show a Timon who still cares enough about man to curse a thief into reformation and to admit that his faithful steward is indeed a good man. Apemantus, then, proves the natural-born, constant, stable satirist, while Timon is the satirist of circumstances.

Having analyzed the catalytic agent, we now come to

[11] Robert C. Elliott, *Power of Satire*, p. 159, calls this a conventional wit-combat in invective, much like that described by Horace in the "Journey to Brundisium."

[12] A significant "syncopation" (Sigurd Burckhardt's term) on the play's socio-economic level: the hereditary nobleman is morally superior to the nouveau-riche type of usurer baronet; Apemantus's cynicism endures while Timon's misanthropy changes with the changing times.

the product of our formula, the fabricated satirist—a compound too volatile to weather the unstable conditions of his situation. In dramatizing "the making and break-ing of the most furious malcontent"[13] in all of his work, Shakespeare depicts the development of a significant sickness. Timon finds a place in L. B. Campbell's view of the Shakespearean tragic hero as slave of one imbalanced passion or humor;[14] the Adlerian, F. Plewa, traces Ti-mon's illness to his vanity, while A. H. Woods and W. I. D. Scott pronounce him suffering from paresis or dementia paralytica.[15] Whatever the malady's label, when used in a stage play it is aesthetically vital that we witness its development—even if it is shown in a formal, stylized manner. Freud's observations on the psychopathic in *Hamlet* can thus be applied to *Timon*:

For the victim of a neurosis is someone into whose conflict we can gain no insight if we first meet it in a fully established state. But, *per contra*, if we recognize the conflict, we forget that he is a sick man, just as, if he himself recognizes it, he ceases to be ill. It would seem to be the dramatist's business to induce the same illness in *us*; and this can best be achieved if we are made to follow the development of the illness along with the sufferer. This will be especially necessary where the repression does not already exist in us but has first to be set up; and this represents a step further than *Hamlet* in the use of neurosis on the stage. If we are faced by an unfamiliar and fully established neurosis, we shall be inclined to send for the doctor (just as we do in real life) and pronounce the character inadmissable to the stage.[16]

[13] O. J. Campbell, *Shakespeare's Satire*, p. 168.

[14] Lily Bess Campbell, *Shakespeare's Tragic Heroes, Slaves of Passion* (1952), p. 83.

[15] These psychoanalytic diagnoses are summarized by Norman N. Holland, *Psychoanalysis and Shakespeare* (1966), pp. 274–275.

[16] Sigmund Freud, "Psychopathic Characters on the Stage" (1962), p. 310.

Timon is fully admissable to the stage. His permit takes the form of the traditions and myths behind the formal satire which was finding a new place on the stage during this period. Timon's first satiric raging comes in the mock feast scene (III, vi) which has roots back in the Old Comedy antecedents of satyr plays.[17] His mock blessing over the covered dishes of water uses the antiprayer to power his first full satiric curse. Accompanied by an appropriately ritualistic act (throwing the water at his victims), the curse rolls out with a traditional satiric precision of detail and rhythm but an ironical twist on the old Greek death call:

> Live loath'd, and long,
> Most smiling, smooth, detested parasites,
> Courteous destroyers, affable wolves, meek bears,
> You fools of fortune, trencher friends, time's flies,
> Cap-and-knee slaves, vapour, and minute-jacks!
>
> (III, vi, 103–107)

In addition to the beast comparisons, Timon includes the Celtic disease wish—"Of man and beast the infinite malady / Crust you quite o'er!"—and finishes with a more modern abstraction: "Burn house! Sink Athens! Henceforth hated be / Of Timon and all humanity!"

Once outside the walls of Athens in the next scene (IV, i), Timon delivers himself of a raging satiric soliloquy in Elizabethan Senecan style; while cursing "Athens" with structured precision, he is really "an enlightened Elizabethan looking back on an Elizabethan London,

---

[17] E.g., Aristophanes' *Acharnians* with feasting as part of the fertility rite; note, also, the cooking episode in Euripides' satyr play, *Cyclops*; this source influence supports the Renaissance notion of satire's Greek origins.

playing seriously with the idea of destroying it,"[18] yet
seeing, even in his mental extremity of passion, that the
destructive weapons will come from man's own self-
seeking nature rather than from myth or magic. Having
just turned satirist, Timon's perceptivity is at its prime;
neurotic stress has not yet brought him to the abyss of
a tragic self-destruction. His speech, a major document
for this study, condemns family structure, judicial, financial, social, sexual and religious customs.

It is carefully structured in four parts. The first (lines
1–15) names, in an incantatory style, specific objects
of his curse: matrons, children, slaves and the very walls
of Athens must revolt; its senators, usurers, slave-holders,
dames and sires all must fall. The second part gener-
alizes the curses, calling in more abstract terms for
"confusion" to permeate all of the city's hitherto well-
ordered institutions:

> *Piety and fear,*
> *Religion to the gods, peace, justice, truth,*
> *Domestic awe, night-rest and neighbourhood,*
> *Instruction, manners, mysteries and trades,*
> *Degrees, observances, customs and laws,*
> *Decline to your confounding contraries*
> *And let confusion live!*

> (IV, i, 15–21)

The third section (lines 21–32) invokes on all he has
named the powerful disease curses of plague, fevers,
sciatica, lust, itches, blains and leprosy. And he concludes by resolving to take action on his views: he will
retreat naked from Athens and constantly invoke the
gods:

[18] James G. Rice, "Shakespeare's Curse" (1947), p. 256.

> *The gods confound (hear me, you good gods all)*
> *Th' Athenians both within and out that wall!*
> *And grant, as Timon grows, his hate may grow*
> *To the whole race of mankind, high and low!*
>
> (37–41)

With an "Amen" he ends his perverse, but not demented, mock prayer.

As we have seen, his wit contest with Apemantus in IV, iii, as well as his dealings with the other visitors in that scene, show Timon still in possession of his faculties, however extreme his neurosis is becoming. Critics have made much of his degeneration in the last part of the play: Elliott finds him "ridiculous" from the point at which he acts the "comic fool" in stoning Apemantus; Campbell finds him mechanical to the point of absurdity in acts IV and V so that his suicide "neither reconciles the destructive forces of his nature nor brings any catharsis to the spectators."[19] These subtle character assessments are undoubtedly correct. Timon, after all, is a hero far more flawed than Antony and finally less admirable than Macbeth. This is largely true because of the difference in the quality of the language these heroes speak.

The language of satire, which is Timon's, can rarely exalt its speaker aesthetically as can the high style of the more conventional tragic hero. Satire's first purpose is to tear down; its tools, though powerful, are low—degrading comparisons, near-comic exclamations, sputtering invectives, low mimetic descriptions. Tragedy, on the other hand, involves the building up of awe and admiration for

[19] Elliott, *Power of Satire*, p. 159; O. J. Campbell, *Shakespeare's Satire*, p. 192.

a trapped human being in part through his own passionate, poetically exalted language. In the "tragical satire" under examination it is natural that the genres should be mixed in some way. But they are not mixed on the linguistic level. Timon speaks in a flatly noble, high-toned style for three acts and then switches abruptly to the language of satire. His "dying" speech begins with his only lyrical lines:

> say to Athens
> Timon hath made his everlasting mansion
> Upon the beached verge of the salt flood,
> Who once a day with his embossed froth
> The turbulent surge shall cover.
>
> (V, i, 217–221)

But it quickly reverts to misanthropic satire:

> Lips, let sour words go by and language end.
> What is amiss, plague and infection mend!
> Graves only be men's works, and death their gain.
>
> (223–225)

Language levels are kept separate, but characterization inevitably becomes a mixture of the satiric and the tragic. While Timon's reactions are almost unbelievably mechanical, and his character belittled by the language he has taken up, nevertheless, his observations on mankind and society have the ring of truth, the authority of a passionate devotion to an ideal. And, after all, the plot does sacrifice him, Shakespeare does "kill" him for a cause.

If some critics have failed to find any catharsis in the play the reason may be that they have been looking for tragic catharsis while the play more strikingly provides a satiric catharsis. It is not pity and terror for the tragic hero which are significantly purged but hatred and censure of man in society. As the satiric hero sacrifices himself, he carries away with him all the hatred and contempt he has aroused in the audience through his insistent railing and raging. Moreover, simultaneously another kind of satiric catharsis—the authorial catharsis discussed early in Chapter I—takes place: by raising his satirist persona to the level of tragic hero, Shakespeare purges his own misanthropic emotions along with those of Timon and the audience.

The play ends with a reconciliation of elements, a purification through sacrifice, a cure after an intensified infection. It becomes Timon's life mission—working from the example of Apemantus—to whip up man's hatred for himself and his institutions, to spread the disease, as it were, of his misanthropy. In so doing he makes himself the nexus of the hatred-censure syndrome and his martyrdom allows a cure of the play's symbolic society to begin. Shakespeare's pessimistic view of the malice of the age, of time and of nature, of an "infected world, is set against that long sickness of life itself which begins to mend at Timon's death."[20] Indeed, Timon's dying curse stresses, at last, the curative aspect of his most virulent satiric attacks: "Plague and infection" are to *mend* "what is amiss," implying that God's scourge will eventually purify humanity of its evils.[21]

[20] Bernard Harris, "Dissent and Satire" (1964), p. 137.
[21] Rice, p. 186, who also suggests that the terrible London plague of 1603 may have influenced the plague curses in *Timon*, *Lear* and *The Tempest*.

Looking forward to death, Timon wishes the Athenian senators the curse of life and adds "Be Alcibiades your plague, you his." His curious relationship with the banished warrior can, I believe, be clarified in terms of its underlying myths and then used to explain the nature of the play's cathartic cure.

The mixture of admiration and opportunism that the younger Alcibiades shows toward the festering, banished Timon (in IV, iii) reminds us of a similar relationship in *Philoctetes* (which appeared about the same time as the first play about Timon, the *Misanthrope* by Phrynicus). Just as young Neoptolemus in Sophocles' play tries to get the valued bow from the diseased Philoctetes, so Alcibiades tries to get support and gold from the raging Timon. Contact with the philosophic recluses seems to improve the moral sensibilities of the young warriors in both cases. In a Christlike way Neoptolemus learns to love and accept the repulsive Philoctetes, while Alcibiades demonstrates a rare mercy in his final selective punishment of Athens. Instead of wreaking blind, total vengeance on the city which had so unjustly banished him (for pleading another's cause), he will punish under the public laws only his proven enemies and Timon's.

As redeemer and avenger, Alcibiades makes his "terrible approach" on Athens and speaks fatefully before he acts to punish the "coward and lascivious town." His speech reestablishes the brunt of the play's satiric criticism which has been voiced by Apemantus and then by Timon:

> *Till now you have gone on and fill'd the time*
> *With all licentious measure, making your wills*
> *The scope of justice. Till now myself and such*

> As slept within the shadow of your power,
> Have wander'd with our travers'd arms and breath'd
> Our suffrance vainly. Now the time is flush,
> When crouching marrow in the bearer strong
> Cries, of itself, "No more!" Now breathless wrong
> Shall sit and pant in your great chairs of ease,
> And pursy insolence shall break his wind
> With fear and horrid flight.

(V, iv, 3–13)

The indolent luxury of Athenian senators (and Jacobean nobility), having been whipped to a fever of financial and moral corruption by satiric flagellation, is now dealt with in the heroic language of righteousness in power. According to the underlying theory of sociological medicine, an excess of irritant eventually cleanses: "Alcibiades' tone helps create a sense of reasserted sanity. The money-madness which has corrupted Athens has been purged in Timon's wild excesses. The fabric of Athenian society is being rewoven."[22]

The satirist in tragedy, like the satirist in comedy (e.g., Jaques), plays the scapegoat who brings about a final mimetic concord. The ambiguous roots of satire explain this paradox but the adaptability of satire to various dramatic forms remains quite at the will of the author. Donald Morrow finds that Shakespeare's tragedies fall into the second of two categories:

The writer of a tragedy not only deals with its cause but he disposes, in one way or another, of his tragic characters. Upon the choice he makes may depend the whole meaning of his work. He can allow his audience to go home still with the taste of tragedy, feeling disturbed, wishing something might be

[22] Elliott, *Power of Satire*, pp. 161–162.

done to remedy the kind of suffering witnessed. Or he may leave it quieted, feeling that the tragedy, harsh as it was, is all over, no problems remaining.[23]

The satiric element in *Timon* supports its tragic structure in such a way as to corroborate this view of Shakespeare's tragedies—even the fiercest of satirical tragedies—as essentially nonrevolutionary. Unlike the satirical forces in *Troilus and Cressida,* the purged emotions at a staging of *Timon of Athens* finally flow inward toward the work of art: instead of stimulating an active audience response, these forces intensify the aesthetic experience. As in another famous late-life tragedy, the author plays out through dramatic action his crucially violent emotions and purges those of the reader, to conclude with "calm of mind, all passion spent."

[23] Donald Morrow, *Where Shakespeare Stood* (1935), pp. 77–78.

7: Conclusion

ONE OF THE more interesting characteristics revealed
in this study of Shakespeare's satirists is what I have
called the conversion motif. Through this device the
author changes a clownlike character's minor carping
into a major dramatic force. A prototype for this motif
may be found in the earliest extant "comedy" of Aristophanes, *The Acharnians* (425 B.C.) in which the main
character is the Old Man and Buffoon, Dikaipolis. After
exposing the sham Thracians (like a later satirist) and
celebrating a country Dionysia (like a true Greek satyr),
he verbally defends himself against the Acharnians' stoning so well that he gains his release and also succeeds in
converting both Half-Chorus and Chorus to his idea of
peace with Sparta.[1]

Shakespeare's most primitive satirist, Margaret of
Anjou, as an aged, deposed queen, shares the Aristo-
phanic buffoon's powerlessness to influence society directly through action. She therefore uses her powerful

[1] My interpretation is based on Francis M. Cornford's commentary on the play in *The Origin of Attic Comedy* (1961), pp.
195 ff. The idea that this Old Comedy should be considered as early
satire is further supported by the fact that it ends with the choric
salute to Dikaipolis in the form of the Song of Archilochus, who
was an infamous primitive satiric curser.

language skills to convert the younger, politically influential women into effective satirists so that her curses eventually, though indirectly, destroy Richard III. The conversion motif becomes thematic in the *Henry IV* plays where so much of the dialogue deals with the very question of the delicately reversible, symbiotic Falstaff-Hal influence. Jaques's notable inability to convert anyone to his own melancholic satire and his envy of the more socially integrated Fool, help to mold him as the comedy's scapegoat. On the other hand, Apemantus's quick success in converting (by example rather than will) the easygoing Timon into a raging satirist is vital to the establishing of Timon as tragic scapegoat. And, as we have seen, Thersites' satiric influence on the whole fabric of *Troilus and Cressida* is geared to avoid creating any one specific satirist (who might then be purged through some variety of the scapegoat mechanism), but rather to infect the other personae, as well as the audience, with his own discontent. Thus the motif of conversion to satire has many varieties, all of which further the satiric forces in the different kinds of plays.

Implicit in the primary satirist's need to work through another character is his traditional inferiority—usually social inferiority due to loss of prestige and money, and/or psychological inferiority caused by an overabundance of the melancholy humors. Margaret and Apemantus best exemplify the social and pecuniary types of inferiority. The latter's cynic philosophy impresses Athenian society only when it is taken over, and literally interpreted, by the renowned nobleman, Timon. Jaques, of course, provides the clearest example of the absurdly melancholic temperament, although Thersites, as well as the others, also demonstrates a marked imbalance of humors: the varieties range from the momentary sadness of Falstaff to the nearly psychopathic rage of Timon. If the audience is to react at all to the primary satirist's message, it must "develop," as Freud explained, the particular melancholic illness of the play: it tends to sympathize with the developing satirist (Hal, Timon) whereas it greets the already established satirist (Falstaff, Apemantus, Jaques, Margaret) with amusement, contempt, or some sort of rejection.

The satirist persona of Renaissance drama falls so readily into the role of the rejected that he is often considered a mere "sick and disappointed man" whose "satire is an abnormal and fallen activity which has no place in a well-ordered society."[2] Just as Aristophanes' buffoon suffered a literal stoning by his society, so later satirists are conventionally abused, rejected or at least satirized in turn. In the earliest Shakespearean play examined, Margaret is satirized only slightly: her curses must remain lethal enough to kill; the play does not elevate her at its conclusion, and her very marked expulsion from the resolution is not necessary. Falstaff's rejection, on the other hand, has dramatic importance: because of his satyric behavior and satiric powers, he is not permitted a place in Henry V's well-ordered society. In production his rejection so easily slips into the scapegoat category that an attendant comic or tragic catharsis may obscure the fact that satiric catharsis is finally stifled in the play.

Jaques, Thersites and Timon are more notably the "sick" satirists of the plays examined. As such, they are

[2] Alvin B. Kernan, *The Cankered Muse* (1959), pp. 250 and 148.

all eligible for the expected rejection, yet they are each treated differently in this respect. Jaques is mocked for his extreme melancholy and finally plays the *pharmakos* very clearly, carrying away satiric censure with him in his exclusion from the romantic plot. Timon, an atypically glorified satirist, i.e., Shakespeare's only satiric hero, is also rejected through his elegantly tragic fall and inability to function in society. Thersites, however, may come in for much literal abuse and criticism in his play, but manages to emerge no more "rejected" than several of the other characters whose nobility was inherited from a strong heroic and chivalric tradition. Thus from the evidence of these plays, the scapegoat means of dramatic rejection assures the working of a satiric catharsis which would make the satiric play a socially admissable vehicle according to Aristotelian standards. Rejection of the satirist without the accompanying purgative effect of the *pharmakos*, on the other hand, does not assure that the play will be a "safe" one for the secure commonwealth such as Plato outlined. And the absence of emphatic rejection of the strong satirist predisposes the drama to an inflammatory effect like that of *Troilus and Cressida*.

Satiric genres are traditionally difficult to define. The Renaissance critic Minturno concluded that dramatic satire must be governed by the rules of either comedy or tragedy.[3] Northrup Frye, however, calls satiric drama a separate, "ironic" form but places it in the mythos of winter, between tragedy and comedy. Comic "discovery," he claims, comes from the audience itself while the analogous judgment in tragedy

[3] Antonio Minturno, *L'arte Poetica*, vol. V (1725), p. 161.

is on the other side of the stage; and whatever it is, it is stronger than the audience. In the ironic play, audience and drama confront each other directly.[4]

Because of satire's intermediate form, then, we must look at the working of satiric catharsis in comparison with the more readily understandable tragic or comic catharsis.

Of the plays examined in this study, the two that have demonstrated the social reconciliation and individual release of comic catharsis are *As You Like It* and *1 Henry IV*. Their satiric elements arouse a much mitigated form of hatred and an oblique censure which are exorcised and purged within the plays. The cathartic release of satire within the two tragedies—*Richard III* and *Timon of Athens*—has depended largely on the working out of the satiric curses. In the former, these are delivered in their primitive, quasi-magical form, while in the latter they have been transmuted to the philosophic cynicisms of an elevated misanthrope satirist of almost neoclassical proportions. I would reserve for Frye's ironic form, *Troilus and Cressida* and *2 Henry IV* where an equilibrium of forces creates the impact of ironic confrontation to the exclusion of satiric catharsis. Satiric emotions of hatred and censure are here aroused but not purged, structurally because of the lack of clear comic or tragic resolution. It is not surprising that the "satyr play" which so interested the Renaissance was claimed as the ancestor of tragicomedy as well as of pastoral drama and satire.[5] Satiric catharsis, as we have seen, does not occur independently of a structural comic or tragic catharsis and the blocking

[4] Northrup Frye, *The Anatomy of Criticism* (1957), p. 289.
[5] Eugene Waith, *The Pattern of Tragicomedy in Beaumont and Fletcher* (1952), p. 50.

of satiric purgation inevitably raises questions about the play's form.

This generic problem brings up a central difficulty with satiric drama, the critical distinction between provocative art and bad art. As we have seen in our discussion of *Troilus and Cressida*, Hegel conjectured that the "social play" with its tragic-comic roots constantly threatened to break away from the category of "true poetry." Similarly, Frye describes the ironic drama as having an arbitrary or meaningless catastrophe: its irony is "difficult to sustain in the theatre because it tends toward a stasis of action."[6] *Troilus and Cressida*, of course, provides our best example of this kind of structure and effect. And the inevitable ensuing critical debate, especially about this play, is whether the stasis comes from an unsuccessful try at comedy or tragedy, or whether the author had some other purpose in mind. I. A. Richards describes this aesthetic effect:

Everyone knows the feeling of freedom, of relief, of increased competence and sanity, that follows any reading in which more than usual order and coherence has been given to our responses. And conversely everybody knows the diminution of energy, the bafflement, the sense of helplessness, which an ill-written, crude, or muddled book, or a badly acted play, will produce, unless the critical task of diagnosis is able to restore equanimity and composure.[7]

We have seen in two of Shakespeare's plays how a feeling similar to Richard's "bafflement" results from the blocking of satiric catharsis; this delicately sustained effect is apt to trouble the audience because it disallows

[6] *Anatomy of Criticism*, p. 285.

[7] Ivor A. Richards, *Principles of Literary Criticism* (1948), p. 235.

the conventional safety-value purpose of art, and, especially on explosive social problems, makes the audience confront the drama directly and unavoidably as a force breaking into their lives outside the theater.[8]

The debated function of the satirist as killer or physician is illuminated by recognition of the mechanism of satiric catharsis. In the plays analyzed, only those satirists who exist in cathartic structures cure their societies, i.e., the representative worlds of their respective dramas. Margaret cures her society by convincing it of her own moral views and purging it of the acknowledged evil. Jaques keeps his play's comic vision pure and healthy by bowing out as its *pharmakos*. And Apemantus indirectly provides a similar sanative scapegoat by influencing Timon to become the play's sacrificial tragic satirist.

In the noncathartic structures of *2 Henry IV* and *Troilus and Cressida*, however, the satirist personae do not cure their societies; instead, they leave them suffering from the satiric exposure of all their weakest joints and wounds. But through Thersites and Falstaff, Shakespeare, as master satirist, works toward the "cure" of actual society by provoking his playgoers to discontent with their lot.

In discussing Aristotle, Plutarch recognized the delicacy of the purgation mechanism and the possibility that it would infect rather than cure:

[8] Berthold Brecht's repudiation of Aristotelian drama in his "Epic Theater" theory is the subject of a work in progress dealing with satiric drama from Aristophanes to the present; Brecht saw that aesthetically alienated theater could stimulate political change and might have to sacrifice that "pleasure" he attributed to Aristotelian purgation; see, *Brecht on Theatre*, ed. John Willett (1964), p. 78.

Hellebore, before it purges, disturbs the body; but if too small a dose be given, it disturbs only and purges not at all; and some taking too little of an opiate are more restless than before; and some taking too much sleep well. Besides, it is probable that this disturbance into which those that are half drunk are put, when it comes to a pitch, conduces to that decay. For a great quantity being taken inflames the body and consumes the frenzy of the mind; as a mournful song and melancholy music at a funeral raises grief at first and forces tears, but as it continues, by little and little it takes away all dismal apprehensions and consumes our sorrows. Thus wine, after it hath heated and disturbed, calms the mind again and quiets the frenzy; and when men are dead drunk their passions are at rest.[9]

A. H. Clough and W. W. Goodwin, eds. (1906), p. 282.

The inhibition of satiric catharsis in a play prevents the audience's aesthetic inebriation and results in a state of anxiety, an aggravated awareness of social ill.

[9] *Plutarch's Essays and Miscellanies*, vol. III, "Symposiacs,"

Bibliography

Aristotle. *Politics.* Translated by H. Rackham. Loeb Library. Cambridge, Mass.: Harvard University Press, 1959.

———. *Rhetoric And Poetics.* Translated by W. Rhys Roberts and Ingram Bywater. Modern Library. New York: Random House, 1954.

Auerbach, Erich. *Mimesis: The Representation of Reality in Western Literature.* Translated by Willard R. Trask. 1953. Reprint New York: Doubleday, 1957.

Babb, Lawrence. *The Elizabethan Malady: A Study of Melancholia in English Literature from 1580 to 1642.* East Lansing, Mich.: Michigan State University Press, 1951.

Barber, Cesar Lombardi. "Saturnalia in the Henriad." In *Shakespeare: Modern Essays in Criticism.* Edited by Leonard F. Dean. 1957. Reprint New York: Oxford University Press, 1961.

———. *Shakespeare's Festive Comedy.* Princeton, N.J.: Princeton University Press, 1959.

———. "The Use of Comedy in *As You Like It*." *Philological Quarterly* 21 (1942): 353–367.

Beet, W. Ernest. "The Oath: New Testament and Christian." In *Encyclopaedia of Religion and Ethics.* Edited by James Hastings. New York: Scribner's, 1961.

Bethell, Samuel L. "The Comic Element in Shakespeare's Histories." *Anglia* 71 (1952): 82–101.

———. *Shakespeare and the Popular Dramatic Tradition.* 1944. Reprint London: Staples Press, 1948.

Brecht, Berthold. *Brecht on Theatre: The Development of an*

Aesthetic. Edited and translated by John Willett. New York: Hill and Wang, 1964.

Burckhardt, Sigurd. *Shakespearean Meanings.* Princeton, N.J.: Princeton University Press, 1968.

Butcher, S. H. *Aristotle's Theory of Poetry and Fine Art: With a Critical Text and Translation of the Poetics.* 4th ed. 1895. Reprint New York: Dover, 1951.

Campbell, Lily Bess. *Shakespeare's Histories: Mirrors of Elizabethan Policy.* 1947. Reprint San Marino, Calif.: Huntington Library, 1958.

———. *Shakespeare's Tragic Heroes, Slaves of Passion.* 1930. Reprint New York: Barnes & Noble, 1952.

Campbell, Oscar James. *Comicall Satyre and Shakespeare's Troilus and Cressida.* Los Angeles: Huntington Library, 1938.

———. *Shakespeare's Satire.* 1943. Reprint Hamden, Conn.: Archon Books, 1963.

Canney, Maurice A. "The Oath: Semitic." In *Encyclopaedia of Religion and Ethics.* Edited by James Hastings. New York: Scribner's, 1961.

Charlton, Henry Buckley. *Shakespearean Tragedy.* 1948. Reprint Cambridge, England: Cambridge University Press, 1961.

Chaudhuri, Sujata. "Shakespeare and the Elizabethan Satire Tradition." In *Shakespeare Commemoration Volume.* Calcutta: Presidency College, 1966.

Clark, Barrett H. *European Theories of the Drama.* New York: Crown, 1965.

Clemen, Wolfgang H. "Anticipation and Foreboding in Shakespeare's Early Histories." *Shakespeare Survey* 6 (1953): 25–35.

Cooper, Lane. *An Aristotelian Theory of Comedy.* New York: Harcourt, Brace, 1922.

Coriat, Isador H., M.D. "The Psychology of Medical Satire." *Annals of Medical History* 3 (1921): 403–407.

Cornford, Francis, M. *The Origin of Attic Comedy.* Garden City, N.Y.: Doubleday, 1961.

Crawley, A. E. "Cursing and Blessing." In *Encyclopaedia of*

Religion and Ethics. Edited by James Hastings. New York: Scribner's, 1961.

Draper, John W. "The Theme of *Timon of Athens.*" *Modern Language Review* 29 (1934): 20–31.

Dryden, John. *Poetical Works of Dryden*. Edited by George R. Noyes. Cambridge, Mass.: Harvard University Press, 1950.

Eckhoff, Lorentz. *Shakespeare: Spokesman of the Third Estate*. Translated by R. I. Christophersen. Oslo Studies in English, No. 3. Oslo, Norway: Oslo University Press, 1954.

Elliott, Robert C. "The Definition of *Satire*: A Note on Method." *Yearbook of Comparative and General Literature*. Bloomington, Ind.: Indiana University Press, 1962.

————. *The Power of Satire: Magic, Ritual, Art*. Princeton, N.J.: Princeton University Press, 1960.

Else, Gerald F. *Aristotle's Poetics: The Argument*. Cambridge, Mass.: Harvard University Press, 1963.

Elyot, Sir Thomas. *The Castell of Helth*. London, 1541.

Euripides. *The Cyclops*. Translated by William Arrowsmith. In *Complete Greek Tragedies*. Edited by David Grene and Richmond Lattimore. Chicago: University of Chicago Press, 1959.

Evans, Bertrand. *Shakespeare's Comedies*. Oxford: Clarendon, 1960.

Feinberg, Leonard. *The Satirist*. Ames, Iowa: Iowa State University Press, 1963.

Fink, Z. S. "Jaques and the Malcontent Traveler." *Philological Quarterly* 14 (1935): 237–252.

Fluchère, Henri. *Shakespeare*. Translated by Guy Hamilton. London: Longmans, 1953.

Frazer, Sir James George. *The Scapegoat*. In *The Golden Bough*, vol. IX. 1913. Reprint London: Macmillan, 1955.

Freud, Sigmund. *Jokes and Their Relation to the Unconscious: Standard Edition of the Complete Psychological Works*, vol. VIII. Edited by James Strachey. 1953. Reprint London: Hogarth Press, 1962.

————. "Psychopathic Characters on the Stage." In *Standard Edition of the Complete Psychological Works*, vol. VII.

Edited by James Strachey. 1953. Reprint London: Hogarth Press, 1962.

Frye, Northrop. *The Anatomy of Criticism*. Princeton, N.J.: Princeton University Press, 1957.

———. "The Argument of Comedy." In *English Institute Essays*. Edited by D. A. Robertson. New York: Columbia University Press, 1948.

Gardner, Helen. "As You Like It." In *More Talking of Shakespeare*. Edited by John Garrett. London: Longmans, 1959.

Goldsmith, Robert Hillis. *Wise Fools in Shakespeare*. 1955. Reprint East Lansing, Mich.: Michigan State University Press, 1963.

Greg, W. W., ed. *Troilus and Cressida, First Folio, 1609*. Oxford: Clarendon, 1951.

Harris, Bernard. "Dissent and Satire." *Shakespeare in His Own Age: Shakespeare Survey 17* (1964): 120–137.

Haydn, Hiram. *The Counter-Renaissance*. New York: Scribner's, 1950.

Hegel, Friedrich. *On Tragedy*. Edited by Anne and Henry Paolucci. Garden City, N.Y.: Doubleday, 1962.

Holland, Norman N. *Psychoanalysis and Shakespeare*. New York: McGraw Hill, 1966.

Horace. *Satires, Epistles and Ars Poetica*. Translated by H. Rushton Fairclough. Loeb Classical Library. Cambridge, Mass.: Harvard University Press, 1961.

Johnson, Edgar. "Satiric Overtones in Shakespeare." In *A Treasury of Satire*. New York: Simon & Schuster, 1945.

Kendall, Paul M. "Inaction and Ambivalence in *Troilus and Cressida*." In *English Studies in Honor of James Southall Wilson*. Charlottesville, Va.: University of Virginia Press, 1951.

Kernan, Alvin B. *The Cankered Muse: Satire of the Eng-Renaissance*. New Haven: Yale University Press, 1959.

———. *The Plot of Satire*. New Haven: Yale University Press, 1965.

Klibansky, Raymond, Erwin Panofsky and Fritz Saxyl. *Saturn and Melancholy*. London: Nelson, 1964.

Kott, Jan. *Shakespeare Our Contemporary.* Garden City, N.Y.: Doubleday, 1964.

Kris, Ernst. *Psychoanalytic Explorations in Art.* New York, International Universities Press, 1952.

Lawrence, William Witherle. *Shakespeare's Problem Comedies.* 1931. Reprint. New York: Frederick Ungar, 1960.

————. "Troilus, Cressida and Thersites." *Modern Language Review* 37 (1942): 422–437.

Lucas, Frank L. *Literature and Psychology.* London: Cassell, 1951.

McNeal, Thomas H. "Margaret of Anjou: Romantic Princess and Troubled Queen." *Shakespeare Quarterly* 9 (1958): 1–10.

Minturno, Antonio. *L'arte Poetica.* Naples, 1725.

Morrow, Donald. *Where Shakespeare Stood: His Part in the Crucial Struggles of His Day.* Milwaukee, Wisc.: University of Wisconsin Press, 1935.

Oliver, H. J. ed. *The Arden Shakespeare: Timon of Athens.* London: Methuen, 1959.

Ornstein, Robert. *The Moral Vision of Jacobean Tragedy.* Madison, Wisc.: University of Wisconsin Press, 1965.

Peter, John D. *Complaint and Satire in Early English Literature.* Oxford: Clarendon, 1956.

Plato. *The Republic.* Translated by F. M. Cornford. New York: Oxford University Press, 1964.

Plutarch. *Essays and Miscellanies,* vol. III. Edited by A. H. Clough and W. W. Goodwin. Boston: 1906.

Popkin, Richard H. *The History of Skepticism From Erasmus to Descartes.* 1960. Reprint Assen, Netherlands: Van Gorcum, 1964.

Puttenham, George. *The Arte of English Poesie.* Edited by Edward Arber. Westminster: Constable, 1895.

Ramsay, G. G., trans. *Juvenal and Persius.* Loeb Classical Library, Cambridge, Mass.: Harvard University Press, 1957.

Randolph, Mary Claire. "Celtic Smiths and Satirists: Partners in Sorcery." *ELH* 8 (1941): 184–197.

————. "The Medical Concept in English Renaissance Satiric Theory." *Studies in Philology* 28 (1941): 125–157.

————. "The Neoclassical Theory of the Formal Verse Satire."
  Ph.D. dissertation, University of North Carolina, 1939.

Reyher, Paul. *Essai Sur les Idées dans l'oeuvre de Shakespeare.*
  Paris: M. Didier, 1947.

Rice, James G. "Shakespeare's Curse: Relation to Elizabethan Tradition and Drama." Ph.D. dissertation, University
  of North Carolina, 1947.

Richards, Ivor A. *Principles of Literary Criticism.* New York:
  Harcourt, Brace, 1948.

Rossiter, Arthur Percival. *Angel With Horns.* New York:
  Theatre Arts Books, 1961.

Schneider, Elisabeth. *Aesthetic Motive.* New York: Macmillan, 1939.

Scott, William Inglis Dunn. *Shakespeare's Melancholics.*
  London: Mills and Boon, 1962.

Shakespeare, William. *The Complete Works.* Edited by George
  Lyman Kittredge. Boston: Ginn, 1936.

Shero, Rogers Lucius. "The Satirist's Apologia." *University
  of Wisconsin Studies in Language and Literature* 15 (1922):
  148–167.

Siegel, Paul N. *Shakespearean Tragedy and the Elizabethan
  Compromise.* New York: New York University Press, 1957.

Spencer, Theodore. "The Elizabethan Malcontent." In *Joseph
  Quincy Adams Memorial Studies.* Edited by James Mc-
  Manaway. Washington: Folger Library, 1948.

Taylor, George C. "Shakespeare's Attitude Towards Love and
  Honor in *Troilus and Cressida.*" *Publications of the Modern
  Language Association* 45 (1930): 781–786.

Tillyard, Eustace M. W. *Shakespeare's History Plays.* New
  York: Macmillan, 1946.

————. *Shakespeare's Problem Plays.* 1950. Reprint London:
  Chatto and Windus, 1961.

Waith, Eugene. *The Pattern of Tragicomedy in Beaumont
  and Fletcher.* Yale Studies in English, No. 120. New Haven:
  Yale University Press, 1952.

Welsford, Enid. *The Fool: His Social and Literary History.*
  1935. Reprint Garden City, N.Y.: Doubleday, 1961.

Wheelwright, Philip. "Catharsis." In *Encyclopedia of Poetry and Poetics.* Edited by A. Preminger. Princeton, N.J.: Princeton University Press, 1965.

Wood, Alice Perry. *The Stage History of Shakespeare's King Richard the Third.* 1909. Reprint New York: AMS Press, 1965.

Index